Dressing the Heart

A Parent's Guide to Everyday Etiquette

A compilation of articles on the subject of Etiquette by

Robin A. Bickerstaff Glover

Christian Living, Etiquette & Character Coach, member AACC

Dedicated to the Glover Girls

Gabe, Noah, Jewell & Selah

Colossians 3

CG Publishing

Applying the Heart and Seeking Wisdom

CG Publishing is the publishing ministry of Christian Graces, LLC. Christian Graces is an organization committed to equipping Christians and families in bible-based spiritual development and child rearing through character, etiquette and Christian coaching and training.

www.christiangraces.com   www.cgpublishing.org

ISBN-13: 978-1475071559
ISBN-10: 1475071558

Cover design by Robin Glover

Unless otherwise noted all Scripture references are taken from the Holy Bible, KJV.

Library of Congress Cataloging-in-Publishing Data

Glover, Robin Bickerstaff.
    The Family Guide to Etiquette/ Robin Bickerstaff
Glover., 1st Edition
    1. Etiquette coaching, 2. Character training.

            Printed in the United States of America

Contents

What is Etiquette?

Defining the Ethics of Etiquette

"Nothing is less important than which fork you use. Etiquette is the science of living. It embraces everything. It is ethics. It is honor."Emily Post

I am very sad to report that there are many people--especially those currently younger than 30 years-- who feel that etiquette is an outdated concept whose time has passed. I want to beg to differ; we need to encourage our young people more now than we ever did before to take up the mantle of social politeness and decorum. Why? Simply put the United States has become a country that values the virtues of culture, style and good moral character, less every year. The great Christian nation is not doing unto others as we would have others do unto us. We who care have to rescue our nation one *'Thank You'* at a time by modeling grace and elegance in our speech, conduct and presentation.

How Can They Show What They Don't Know?

Education is always the first step to transformation. You cannot implement ideas, thoughts and concepts to which you have neither been introduced nor taught. As a first step then I would like to introduce the definitions and applications within the subject of Etiquette. After all we cannot show what we do not know!

Let's begin with some basic definitions and information on the origins of the term etiquette.

- The word *Etiquette* derives from the French *estiqu* meaning to attach or stick.
- It is a noun which describes conventional requirements as to social behavior; proprieties of conduct as established in any class or community or for any occasion.
- A prescribed or accepted code of usage in matters of ceremony, as at a court or in official or other formal observances.
- The code of ethical behavior regarding professional practice or action among the members of a profession in their dealings with each other: medical etiquette. [1]

What Does it All Mean?

Etiquette is the fruit of manners and it deals directly with kindness, consideration, elegance, style and decorum. Here are some quick tips to start you on the road to social grace.

- Before you do something ask yourself, "What is the kindest way to do this?"
- Etiquette involves putting others first but not necessarily putting yourselves down.
- Etiquette should flow out of a gracious and kind heart and not be rigidly followed like a set of commandments. Etiquette is realized then caught.
- Etiquette customs may vary from one culture to another so as the saying goes 'when in Rome…well you know the rest.
- Social etiquette is the most common form of etiquette and it involves social graces.

Basic Manners

What Does It Mean To Be Mannerly

Manners Check-up

They are easy to spot and hard to forget. This is the truth of all well-mannered individuals, be they man, woman, boy or girl. The truth is that the mannerly person stands out in a crowd. When you meet him or her you are immediately impressed by his or her charming and magnetic personality. The great news is that manners are taught and anyone can become well-mannered if they sincerely seek to do so.

You may have noticed, whether at work, home or play, that the people who are well-respected and whom others want to be around are generally mannerly, respectful and well-socialized. This is because the mannerly person lives by what is commonly referred to as the *'Golden Rule'* and they sincerely seek to do good unto others as much as possible.

What does it mean then, to be mannerly? It means that the person is warm and genuine, with a commitment to being considerate and kind to others.

The mannerly person is known by the fruit of his or her characteristics and values. How about a manners checkup?

The mannerly person exhibits **self-confidence.** This character trait is usually observed through their behavior and savvy way of interacting in both social and business situations. Upon meeting the mannerly person, you will be impressed by his or her adeptness and ability to comfortably navigate circumstances, whether familiar or not. Just remember that learning to be confident in what you stand for and in your abilities does not necessarily demand that you become proud and obnoxious. On the contrary, people are attracted to power constrained by humility and wielded for purpose not gain.

When a person is mannerly, she is **considerate** of others. Her sensitivity toward the plight or difficulties of others, dictates that she not only notice, but that she also does whatever necessary to meet their needs. Mannerly children are ever aware that their behavior reflects their upbringing and as a result, they are thoughtful and courteous representatives of their home when they are with others.

The mannerly person is purposely aware of the rights of others. He is **respectful** in his associations, recognizing differences whether these be due to age, culture, or status. In any given situation he shows due deference and obsequiously respects the young and old alike. Recognizing position, he is also quick to show obeisance without seeming phony.

When you meet a person of impeccable manners, you will most likely find her to be a very practical problem-solver who has an uncanny **common sense** style. This is the person who knows when to remain silent and when to speak up on a matter. She is able to maintain relationships through her commitment to integrity and she is a go-to confidante who gives wise advice.

A person of great manners uses **tact,** values honesty and understands the power of words and actions. Because he does, he will generally be slow to respond and will purposely act, rather than react to most situations. He is careful to think before he speaks or acts and this is accounted to him as gracious behavior by his family, friends and co-workers. As you grow in etiquette, remember not to allow your biases and opinions to draw you away into vain and corrupting conversations. Have and maintain convictions, but pick your battles.

Flexibility is another of the well-mannered person's character traits. It is true that you will find most mannerly people to be somewhat traditional; however, he or she is also one that recognizes that there are necessary accommodations and modifications that must be made in the name of etiquette and for the sake of cultural sensitivity. It is not necessarily true that he or she will appreciate change just for the sake of personal conveniences; however, he or she is normally comfortable with changes that are solution driven and aimed at enhancing everyday life.

How did you do? As you assess your manners quotient remember that manners can be learned and even mastered at any age. While it is true that when taught in childhood, manners become foundational building blocks for good habits, relationships, work ethics, learning and growing, take heart and know that it is never too late to improve upon your manners.

It is also important to remember that cultivating good manners is not a limiting factor which requires stoic behavior or prevents deep thinking and absent-mindedness. On the contrary, developing good manners is actually a great way to enhance your own unique personality traits and style. The shy person is helped by her etiquette training to overcome the fear of relating to others and thus she presses through this tendency out of politeness and concern for others. If you are a person who loves to disagree, good manners will equip you to be agreeable and pleasant as you disagree. Perhaps one of the most important benefits of perfecting good manners is evident within the family and home. When you are well-mannered, your respectful, considerate, tactful, practical and flexible behavior will go a long way toward encouraging your loved ones and cementing the bonds of love and respect within your home sweet home.

Manners at Mealtime

Lessons for Children

Mealtime Etiquette for children (and many adults) is very important. Why? This is a hot topic because so many people get nervous and upset when invited to a meal because they are unsure about their etiquette and manners. Let's look at some basic etiquette rules for dining. There are many great resources including Emily Post's book *The Guide to Good Manners for Kids, offers some great advice for children at mealtime.*

Here are seven quick tips toward enjoying more mannerly dining

Before you sit down to eat, wash your hands and face. Have you made it a habit to wash up before meals? There are so many opportunities to become ill due to dirty hands. Make a real effort to incorporate this as a habit in your life and make sure that your children emulate your behavior

No one should begin eating until everyone is seated and the hostess begins to eat. This is a common courtesy which shows respect for the hostess/host. It really is very rude to sit down and begin enjoying the meal while the cook or host is still bringing in more food or preparing to enjoy the meal and the fellowship along with his or her family or guests.

Be positive and grateful about the food. Teach your children not to complain about the food choices. This is a common problem. Children like to eat what they like to eat-and not much more. Teach them to compliment the host/hostess on what they like or to remain silent about what they do not. Cooking is a labor of love. Help them understand the importance of being appreciative.

Everyone at the table should be included in the conversation. This is a great opportunity for your children to work on their communication skills. Communication involves listening, speaking and understanding. Encourage them to speak up, to ask questions and to listen when others are sharing. You want them to understand that they should not monopolize the conversation; however they must learn to be a part of it.

Keep yourself presentable. Make sure your children understand that they should use their napkin to wipe their face if needed. In addition, they should keep their hands clean and try not to make a mess around their plate area. This can be difficult for some children so just remember to encourage their efforts and practice, practice, practice.

No rude or inappropriate behavior. These might include anything from loud belching to eating with food in their mouth. Explain that proper manners are born out of the desire to help others feel comfortable. These behaviors will do just the opposite.

Give proper thanks. Even if you are a part of a household that does not offer a pre-meal blessing, there should always be thanks given during the meal. Teach your children to thank the cook (even if that is you) and to make this a matter of habit in life. Sometimes preparing meals can seem a thankless task for moms and dads. This brings us to one of my 'fabulous five' sayings which just happens to be, 'Thank you.'

Make practicing manners a daily habit at home and when you are dining out. Your children will be grateful to you for the training in later years. Great manners are a large part of your personal presentation arsenal.

Manners & Civility

This section offers information on Basic manners and Civility. It includes articles that deal with subjects such as business and workplace etiquette, how to behave like a gentleman (or lady), developing personal style and attire, and following proper decorum and protocol in both your public and interpersonal communication interactions.

Social Etiquette on Casual

The word 'casual' is over-used or perhaps abused in our current day. This usage is usually accompanied by an attitude that lacks any adherence to convention or formality. Casual used to imply a reprieve or holiday from the usual formalities one observed. That said, in order for something to be casual, it must contrast the normal state of being which is formality. In our current culture, casual has become the norm leaving one to ask if the term is even necessary anymore? Miss Manners writes about the overuse of casual in her "Guide to Domestic Tranquility" book.

"Instead, Casual became a religion. It must now be one of the most zealously overused terms we have. One hears all the time of Casual clothes, Casual meals, casual entertaining, Casual attitudes and even dedicated Casual people." (Martin, pg 235)

With all of this in mind, it is important (as people interested in etiquette and in doing what is right and best for all involved) that we understand how *casual* currently looks and what we can do in order to turn the tide. We want to influence the culture toward excellence and formality because one of the first things to disappear in any crumbling relationship is consideration or respect. Casual attitudes and behaviors tend to take others for granted and to not esteem others as highly as we ought. Let us then consider how to spot the "Casual" and remove it where it is not necessary.

The Casual meal. This is the get together that is characterized by paper plates, disposable table cloths, paper towels and food that is easily tossed after the meal. This meal is usually quick and easy to prepare and without a doubt it has a place. This should not be our norm however. Ordinarily, when we invite others to our home in order to dine with us they should feel a bit fussed over. This should be a special occasion and we should endeavor to put our best foot forward by entertaining and receiving them with grace and style.

Casual Clothing. The idea of Casual clothing connotes ease and comfort; the message relayed is that the article feels better on than it looks. We have seen the perpetuation of the wannabe Casual dress on Fridays in the business world. These items are usually more expensive than they look and still acknowledged as a break away from the normal more formal business dress that is expected during the other four business days of the week.

Casual Entertaining. As sad as it seems, there are those who do what they call casual entertaining. In this situation neither the host nor the guest is interested or motivated in creating an atmosphere that is entertaining. There is usually no agenda and no one takes an active responsibility to make things happen. The evening simply is. Eventually, the guests go home and the evening is concluded. This type of entertaining should not be a goal for the socially savvy. At the very least as a host or hostess you should have a loose plan for the evening even if it is only a plan to discuss what the group should do next. I must share with you that this is not truly entertaining.

Casual People. We have all known a Casual person. He or she is the one who has no intentions of exerting any energy and who might be viewed as lazy, under-motivated or a drop-out. I would encourage you to avoid gaining such a reputation unless you are independently wealthy and have no need of other people at all! Seriously, it is very difficult to abide a dead-beat so I would encourage you to be diligent in your livelihood and daily pursuits. You will be seen as a person of integrity and sought after as someone to be emulated and admired. Hard work really is a hallmark of good character.

Casual Attitude. Perhaps one of the worse in this category has to be the Casual attitude. This is the attitude usually attributed to rebellious young adults that says nothing or none of this (including you) really matters very much at all. The truth is most of your choices in life really do have immense meaning to both you and those in your life. This is an attitude that is best suited for lazy Saturday afternoons, vacations and holidays. During the formal days of work, school, church and more we should be dedicated to committing ourselves to a determined attitude that pursues excellence.

Casual used to carry with it a certain dignity all its own. It was the easygoing choice at approved times within our normal, more formal, living. Deliver the Casual meal using simple foods but in the same respectful manner as you would a four-course steak meal. Do this by using platters rather than card board cartons and metal rather than plastic. When dressing casually remember that your clothing should still be appropriate for the situation, clean and attractive. There is never any excuse to look like a vagabond unless you are auditioning for a role in a play! Yes, there is something to be said for the Casual occasion's spontaneity. These may be low key and informal but your guests convenience and comfort should never be compromised.

Etiquette does not attempt to bind individuals to a set of rules. Instead, as you use etiquette to navigate your life, you will find that you operate in an ease that exudes confidence and poise. Others will admire your well-meaning and considerate behavior and you will be highly respected for your sensitivity to your friends, family and colleagues.

References: Miss Manners' Guide to Domestic Tranquility, Judith Martin.1999

Behaving Well: Manners Tips For Men

Considerate, Respectful and Honest.

Although etiquette is unique and separate from principles, they are necessarily connected. Etiquette is the collection of manners that a society formulates specifically for the purpose of getting along well together. This etiquette is then guided by three basic principles which include consideration, respect and honesty. Surveys show that when a man shows and treats others with respect his image stands out and he is regarded as not only a person of good manners but as one to be highly valued by others.

In order to understand and practice good etiquette it is important to understand the governing principles mentioned above. **consideration, respect,** and **honesty** are all three characteristic traits that transcend culture, age and economic status. He who commits to practice etiquette will find himself more confident and prepared in most any situation he encounters. His reputation will precede him and he will be known as a gentleman who does things correctly, behaves honorably and knows why to do what he does.

In order to lay the proper foundation for this commitment to principled living, here are some basic definitions concerning the value and character of consideration, respect and honesty.

- **A look at Consideration.** According to the online resource Dictionary.com, the word *Consideration* is from the late 14c., "a beholding, looking at," also "keeping in mind," from Fr. considération (12c.), from L. considerationem, noun of action from consider are (see consider). Meaning "a taking into account" is from c.1460; that of "something given in payment" is from c.1600. Its definitions include: noun 1. The act of considering; careful thought; meditation; deliberation: I will give your project full consideration. 2. Something that is or is to be kept in mind in making a decision, evaluating facts, etc.: Age was an important consideration in the decision. 3. Thoughtful or sympathetic regard or respect; thoughtfulness for others: They showed no consideration for his feelings. 4. a thought or reflection; an opinion based upon reflection. 5. a recompense or payment, as for work done; compensation.

The considerate gentleman is one who is thoughtful, kind, respectful and deliberate in his behaviors. He will not be known as a spontaneously rash or excitable person, but as one who is in control and acts in accordance with his kind intentions. Etiquette expert, Peter Post reminds us that the considerate person is mindful of how other people and entities are affecting by whatever is taking place. Once the considerate gentleman or lady has assessed how the situation will affect all involved he or she is clear on how to proceed.

- **Considering Respect.** The word respect originated around 1300–50; (noun) Middle English (< Old French) < Latin respectus action of looking back, consideration, regard, equivalent to respec-, variant stem of respicere to look back (re- re- + specere to look) + -tus suffix of v. action; (v.) < Latin respectus past participle of respicere (Dictionary.com) Although the word is closely associated with consideration it does connote a trait very different. Respect is defined many times with relation to how one regards another person or entity. The person who is respectful shows esteem for or a sense of the worth or excellence of a person, a personal quality or ability, or something considered as a manifestation of a personal quality or ability: **I have great respect for her judgment.** or one who acknowledges and gives deference to a right, privilege, privileged position, or someone or something considered to have certain rights or privileges; proper acceptance or courtesy; acknowledgment: respect for a suspect's right to counsel; to show respect for the flag; respect for the elderly. Respect is also the condition of being esteemed or honored: to be held in respect. When a gentleman shows respect he is then careful to make sound judgements on how to pursue relationships and on how to approach other individuals. A person of etiquette will show this respect for others regardless of the person's status or appearance. There ought always be respect given to others by default.

Holding to Honesty. The word honesty originated in or around early 14c., from O.Fr. honesté, from L. honestatem (nom. honestas) "honor, honesty," from honestus (see honest). In English, the word originally had more to do with honor than honest. (dictionary.com) This word and character trait has to do with a person's uprightness. It is defined as a noun, meaning the quality or fact of being honest; uprightness and fairness,truthfulness, sincerity, or frankness and a freedom from deceit or fraud. The gentlemen does not find it necessary to be what might be termed brutally honest but he is sincere in his communications. Rather than blasting someone with an accusation such as, "You don't know what you're talking about." the gentlemen would instead reply, "I don't happen to agree with what you are saying." Honesty which shows both consideration and respect.

Invitations

Invitation Etiquette and Party Manners Advice.

Formal Invitation Etiquette

Tips on the Art of Inviting

Creating the perfect invitation

Many people, who rarely consider matters of etiquette in their everyday lives, tend to be very concerned about etiquette and proper form when it comes to sending, receiving and responding to written invitations. While beautiful engraving and excellent penmanship are both wonderful to display on your invites, there are four things that the proper invitation must include. These four invitation necessities are the: who, why, when and where of the event.

For the most formal social situations:

If at all possible your invitations should be hand-written or engraved. Use formal wording. Here is an example:

> *Elizabeth Jewell and Gabriella Daniels* (**who**)
> *request the pleasure of Judith Walker's company*
> *at dinner* (**why**)
> *on Saturday,February eighteenth,*
> *at seven o'clock* (**when**)
> *7 Evenstar Place,* (**where**)
> *RSVP*
> *123-555-1111*

Variations abound and they will enable you to adjust the level of formality used in your invitation. For example, instead of using *"request the pleasure"* use *"invite you to."* Instead of using the third person reference, you can use the pronoun "you" and drop the "company" in the above wording. These and similar changes will give you a less formal invitation while still giving your invited guests all of the necessary information.

Plan ahead and extend your invitations as far in advance as you are able

Save-the-date cards are fine and should be used when the event is scheduled for several months or a year in the future.

Make every effort to have the correct information including the right time and day on your invites. If this requires that you wait an extra week or so for confirmation, then wait the extra week if you can. Remember, the first information your guests receive will stick with them even if you have to make changes in the future.

Your invitations should match the level of formality and they should complement the style of your event.

Choosing to use a calligrapher or pay for expensive engraving is not necessary in most situations. However, if you are planning an extremely formal affair you may want to consider the grand presentation either of these might add to your invitations.

For informal events, small dinner parties and other more casual events, you may certainly use handwritten informal notes, telephone calls or pre-printed store bought invitations.

Be creative with your invites. Keep in mind that there are no hard and fast rules about invitations except that they should always include the essential information listed above.

For very informal get-togethers you may simply want to offer an email or verbal invite to your friends, family or colleagues.

Offer your invited guests hints in your language and wording. More formal invites use subjunctive case grammatical clues. These are identified by the presence of verb tenses moved back in time. For instance, instead of *"May I"* the more formal invite will read *"Might I."*

Gift and money matters.

I know it is a popular thing for brides and mothers-to-be to do in our culture, however, listing registry information or gift suggestions on your invitation is wrong. Many people are put off by what they perceive the greedy nature of such information.

If your event is a fundraiser it is perfectly acceptable (and expected) that you mention money and or donations in your invitation package.

For gatherings, weddings or showers where gifts are appropriate, interested guests can ask for registry information when they respond to the invite. It is also fine for your guests to ask a close relative or friend for gift suggestions and/or registry information if they would like.

In general you should try to avoid prohibitive language including the increasingly common *"no gifts please"* notice.

It is considered in poor taste to request money or cash in your invitations.

If you are the recipient of an invitation that offers gift suggestions, it is perfectly fine for you to totally ignore the information.

What is the appropriate response to a mailed or telephoned dinner invitation from either a friend or acquaintance?

Question: *What Should I Do If I Receive A Formal Dinner Invitation?* *"I just received an invitation to a dinner party and I don't know the hostess very well. Please list some helpful tips on what to do next."*

Answer:

Dinner parties are great fun. They offer a chance to get out and interact with your friends and loved ones, meet new people and of course try delicious new food. When you are invited remember that there are some specific guests 'no-no's to keep in mind.

Once you have received an invitation to dinner **and** you have checked your calendar to make sure you are available you should **respond to the host.** This may be done either by mail, telephone or email if you like. During your conversation remember that this is not your dinner party and you should not specify any food likes, preferences or dislikes. Ask if there is any way you might be helpful and if you are uncertain of the attire for the evening, ask. A dinner party is a great time to wear some of your more dressy outfits. Once you know the type of dinner, you may have a better idea of what to wear. Once you have decided, pull out all the stops and do your best to look good. Be stylish and elegant but, remember to consider your comfort. There seems to be a direct correlation between hurting feet and a bad attitude. Remember, you want to be a great guest who is pleasant to be around.

Arrive to the dinner on time. Once you are there prepare to abide by the host's agenda. **Sit according to the place card directions** and don't be fussy about the arrangements. If you happen to be served something that you cannot or do not eat, simply eat around it without comment.

Wait for the host or person of honor to begin eating before you do. If someone asks you to pass a particular dish, set it beside the next person's plate asking them to pass it to the person. This continues person to person until it arrives at the original requester.

When all is said and done, don't forget to **have a great time.** After the party a nice thank you note is appropriate thus letting the host know just how much you enjoyed the evening.

Party Invitation Etiquette

Everyone loves receiving party invitations and it is great fun preparing for an especially unique or momentous event. Follow these quick guidelines and your host or hostess will be glad you were on his or her list!

What to do once you receive a party invitation:

The first thing you should do once you have received a party invitation is **check your calendar.** This will enable you to avoid a last minute cancellation due to an over looked prior engagement. Although you might disappoint the party host if you're unavailable, you will do them a favor if you plan to attend and set aside the date for their event as soon as you know about it.

Next, **respond to the invite.** Responding promptly is helpful for planning purposes and highlights your gracious nature. If you wait too long to respond it may appear that you either don't want to come or are waiting to make sure you don't get a better offer. Either option is objectionable so decide whether you will or will not go and respond accordingly.

Assume you are able to **bring a guest.** If the invitation is unclear on this point, contact the host and ask whether you may.

Bring a Gift. Your host will appreciate the nice gesture. If this is an outdoor picnic why not pick up some extra cans of soda or bags of chips.

In general, abide by the invitation's instructions. **Call ahead with questions**. It is preferable to ask beforehand than to show up and create and awkward situation that was totally preventable. Consider calling ahead when the attire is not specified. You would hate to show up in swim wear and a cover-up to a formal dinner party! When in doubt it is best to ask.

Finally, let your host know how much you enjoyed the party. **Send a Thank You note.** Remember that big parties and events require a lot of work. Just imagine your friend or colleague's surprise when you actually acknowledge their efforts and success at entertaining well.

Have fun and remember that it is not difficult to be a great party guest. Simply take the time to be considerate and kind and you will go a long way towards being regarded as a class act/must have party guest.

Save the Date

Do you ever wonder what is expected of you when you receive a 'Save the Date' invitation to a party or event? Here are some tips on how to respond before the party and after.

First **check your calendar.** If you intend to take your spouse or significant other along it is a good idea to check with them about their availability too. This will enable you to make a confident decision and 'save the date' for your friend's special occasion.

Next be sure to **respond to the invite promptly.** A delayed response may be misinterpreted by your friend or colleague. Your potential host might assume you are not interested or are waiting to see if you might get a more appealing offer. Be considerate and let them know your intentions as soon as possible.

Read the instructions carefully. Make sure you have the correct information and if you have questions by all means call ahead to be sure. These questions might concern whether or not a meal will be served, the desired attire for the occasion or whether gifts are okay to bring.

Bring a party help. For a formal dinner party you might want to bring your host some flowers or you can bring soda and chips to a picnic.

Have fun! Your host thought you would be a great addition to his or her party-don't disappoint, be yourself and enjoy the party.

Don't forget to **thank your host.** This may be done either in person or by the sending of a short note after the event. Parties and events require a lot of work and your host will be so grateful to receive some feedback on his or her efforts.

Parties are so exciting. Don't get over anxious about attending. Remember if your friend didn't believe you'd be an asset to the event you probably wouldn't have been invited.

May I bring along an uninvited guest?

Question: *What Should I Do If My Children Aren't Named on the Wedding Invitation?*

I recently received a wedding invitation from a family friend. I noticed that the envelope only mentions my husband's and my name. Will it be okay to take them along anyway? They are very well behaved.

Answer:

Quite often couples are choosing to have more elaborate and therefore costly wedding ceremonies and receptions. Many families are finding their children have not been invited to these events and have questions about how to handle the invite.

The outer envelope of a formal envelope will traditionally only name the parents of the family. Check the inner envelope to see if perhaps your children are named there. If they are not then you may still have a few options. This could be an oversight. If you feel close enough you could check with your friend's parent or close friend to see if perhaps the couple has made the decision to not invite children to the wedding. If this is the case you should simply make the decision to either attend or not. If you happen to have the opportunity to speak with the bride or groom yourself you might want to ask if the children were invited. This could prove an awkward situation, so I would caution against this option.

In general most brides put a lot of time into their guest list. If your children were not included on the invitation, it is probably best that you not take them to the wedding.

Wedding Invitation Etiquette

The wedding invitation is often the first sample your guests will have of your upcoming celebration. With that in mind it is very important that your invites represent the type of wedding you are planning as well as the mood you hope to set. For instance, if you are having a very formal (white tie) evening ceremony you would not want to mail out copied invites on bright card stock paper with a smiley face on the envelope. Instead, your mailing would be on fine stationer's paper, with engraved or thermo-engraved print. You may even want to finish them off with satin ribbons or some other classic embellishment to set it apart from the rest.

Remember that you are going for an overall impression beginning with your announcements and finishing with your thank you notes. The wording on the invite should be carefully thought out and you should be sure to use proper etiquette during the mailing. Decide with your parents (if they are sending the invitations) how they would like to be acknowledged. Some parents who have divorced may want their names omitted from the invites. This is a sensitive issue and definitely the subject for another article. Suffice it to say that this issue should be given careful thought. This would include making sure your titles are correct and that you have arranged the family names in order.

Here are some points to keep in mind when you are addressing your wedding invitations.

Begin with a complete list. Your list should contain all of the names of your invited guests. This should include the children, if they are invited, and any other family members living within the same household.

Separate the invites by family. If there is more than one family living in a household, each should receive their own personal invitation. For instance, there should be one addressed to *'Mr. and Mrs. Roderick Frazelton'* and another to *'Miss Sharon Dempsey.'*

Practice your handwriting. Invitations can be very costly and most people do not buy many extras. For this reason, it is wise to practice your handwriting on a sheet of paper before you begin the activity of addressing your envelopes.

Use proper addressing. The inside envelope should list the individual names of the invitees, while the outside envelope should be addressed to the head of the household and family. The return address should be listed either in the upper left hand corner of the envelope or on the flap of the sealed envelope. An example might read something like this. On the outer envelope you would write:

"Mr. and Mrs. Matthew P. Hamilton, 1234 Rosenblum Circle, Fairfax, Virginia 21045."

The inner envelope would then read:

"Matthew, Mary, Melvin and Martha Hamilton."

Here is another example. To a single invited guest you would write:

"Miss Judith R. Hanks, 1234 Arlington Boulevard, Indianapolis, Indiana 46205."

Her inner envelope could then read:

"Judith and Guest."

Stamp your RSVP cards. If you are requesting a response to the invitation by mail then you should include the response card, along with a stamped and addressed envelope. This will make receiving your responses convenient while at the same time show courtesy on your part.

Just the facts. Your invitations should not include such things as registration information or gift suggestions. If a guest needs to know this information they should be able to call you or a family member. This should not be a part of the invitation.

This is just some basic information to get you well on your way to getting a proper invitation in the mail. Make sure you use black ink and take care to hand stamp the invitations. This is a great activity for you, your mother and your maid of honor to conquer together on a lazy Saturday afternoon.

Wedding Etiquette

The Wedding Etiquette section deals with everyday and common questions and concerns that wedding guests and attendants may have.

Wedding Invitation Guest List Questions

Creating the perfect wedding guest list

Your wedding may just be one of the most exciting days of your life. I certainly hope it was or will be an experience you will never forget. This should be a time that is magical and beautifully special. In your efforts to present the best wedding ceremony and celebration effort you should definitely tie everything you do together by theme and level of formality. This includes your choice of wedding invitation wording, paper and even method of printing.

The wedding invitation may be the first glimpse your guests have of the impending celebration's style. If you have already mailed out engagement announcements these should be on the same level of formality and style. Remember for many friends and family members, your announcements, invitations, and programs will serve as mementos of your big day; you want to make a statement with everything you create for your wedding day.

Here are some common answers to questions couples face when they are preparing their wedding invitations guest list.

The bride's family is paying... does that mean she gets to invite more guests? This decision should be made by the couple together with their parents. In general, the bride's family may decide on the number of guests to be invited, but the groom's family should be allotted a minimum of half of the guests spots.

What should I do about a disapproving mother-in-law to be? Should we allow her to come anyway? Absolutely, under most circumstances your parents should be invited to the wedding. If she has chosen to do something odd like wear a black dress or mourning cap to display her feelings, let her. Think of how she will feel years later when she sees the wedding photos and realizes how foolish she was to attempt to ruin your wedding day.

Do I have to allow my single friends to bring a guest? You do not have to allow your single guests to bring along a friend. If this person is involved in a long-term, committed relationship of which you aware, it would be courteous of you to invite both and this person should then receive his or her own personalized wedding invitation to the ceremony.

How do I stop our mothers from adding guests to our list? This is a very proud time for mothers and fathers. Often mothers feel a part of the celebration so much so that they get overly excited and tend to invite all of their friends and colleagues. The best remedy to this problem is for you and your fiancé to have a loving talk with your mothers and gently but firmly reiterate that the guest list has been established and that they should not invite any more guests.

Do I have to invite my fiancé's ex...? *My soon-to-be five-year old step-daughter will be a part of the ceremony; how should I handle her whether or not to invite her mom?* This would probably be uncomfortable for you and your fiancé. The best solution would be to have a designated person to see to the child's care during the ceremony and immediately after and opt to not invite the mom.

Is it appropriate to send invitations to those I know won't be able to attend? *I don't want them to think I am just trying to solicit a wedding gift.* You should definitely send invitations to your close friends, family members and anyone else you would like to attend your ceremony and celebration. If they are unable to attend so be it, but it will not be because they were not invited. You might just be surprised and they may be there with bells on.

Do I have to invite my bridesmaid's parents? Although your bridesmaids might expect their parents to be invited, if your guests list is limited you might just need to explain that you were unable to do so. If you have known the family for a long time and are very close to them then you definitely should find a way to include these parents.

May I only invite some children and restrict others? Unless a particular child is a part of the wedding party, you should deal with all of the children involved in the same manner. It would be rude to inform your other guests that their children are not invited and then they arrive only to see other children who are not in the wedding party at the celebration.

What is the rule on close relations? Do I have to invite a close relation if we have not spoken in years? You should be kind and invite this relative just as you are the rest of the family. The rule of etiquette is that you deal kindly and mannerly with others and do the right thing. Invite your estranged relative and if he or she comes great; if they don't come, then your conscience is clear.

Engagement Etiquette

Tips for the newly engaged couple.

After a time of courting, dating or getting to know one another, couples who have decided there is no living without the other usually decide to marry. The first big event on the road to the ceremony is the engagement. Here are some tips for the bride and groom-to-be on the etiquette of being and getting engaged.

> **Making the announcement.** As a sign of respect, your parents should be the first to know about your impending nuptials; this is true regardless of your age. If they have already been introduced this is easier. However, if your parents have not met your fiancé, it would be best to visit their home where you can introduce them face to face. If you are concerned about one set of parents learning the news before the other, a nice compromise might be to arrange for the six of you to meet at a nice restaurant where you can make the announcement to both sets at once. You may be tempted to tell your siblings first, but remember your parents are responsible for bringing you into this world, so they ought to be respected with the right of first knowledge. Traditionally the order is: parents, siblings, grandparents, aunts, uncles, close friends then cousins. **For the parent,** if you have recently met your son or daughter's intended, it would be polite of you to send him (or her) an acknowledgement note welcoming him/her to the family.

> **What about my children?** Your children should definitely be among the first to know. If you have been married before or already have children, recognize early on that this could be a scary and potentially anxious time for them. Respect your child's rights and feelings by letting arranging a private time for the two (or more) of you to discuss your engagement and marriage plans. Your fiancé should probably not be involved in your initial conversation with your children. This will give you the opportunity to answer any question he/she or they

might have and to alleviate any anxiety they might have about the changes that are about to occur in their lives and to their relationship with you.

Do I have to tell my former spouse? You should definitely tell your former spouse about your engagement. If you are still on friendly terms, this conversation should be take place in person if at all possible. In addition to showing your former spouse respect, if children are involved it will give him or her the opportunity to ask questions about potential changes with regard to any custody and visitation arrangements. For instance, you should address specific situations such as your custody of any minor children and the spouse's visitation rights, in particular be sure to address any changes you anticipate after you are re-married.

How long should my engagement last? There are many factors that may determine the length of your engagement. Traditionally, this time period lasted around six-months. However, depending upon the style and degree of formality that you are planning your wedding may take longer to coordinate. There are other circumstances that may delay your wedding day as well. These include such variables as the availability of your reception hall and caterer, or the prescribed pre-nuptial counseling required by your church or the person who will officiate during your ceremony. Some more popular ceremony or reception locations may be reserved for up to two years or more. Planning to have a wedding in the less popular fall or winter months may offer more availability and fewer obstacles. There is also the issue of paying for your big day and the honeymoon. All of these should be discussed and budgeted for together so that you are able to begin your married lives together without the stress and strain of excessive financial debt.

Writing Great Wedding Thank You Cards

Every wedding gift deserves a note of thanks.

In general everyone who was in anyway involved in making your wedding a success should be thanked with a personalized, handwritten letter of thanks. These are too numerous to name, however here are some of the people you definitely don't want to forget.

Your Parents. Don't forget to send a note of thanks to both sets of parents and should your family include a step-parent, he or she should receive a note too. Dependent upon how much your celebration costs them, you might want to do something even more.

Your Attendants and Groomsmen. These who stood or will stand with you on your big day certainly deserve a note of thanks as well as a token gift that expresses your gratitude. Include a photo of him or her with you and your spouse as an extra personal touch.

The Officiant. Your minister or officiant has probably spent many hours with you and your spouse in counseling and preparation. Although this is often a paid service, you will also want to send a note of thanks to show your appreciation.

The Wedding Planner. So many of us would have been lost on our wedding day without the help of our event or wedding planner. Make sure he or she is thanked appropriately with a sincere and handwritten note; it is much deserved.

Guests. It is not necessary to send a note of thanks to each person who attended your wedding. You will want to send a thank you note to those who gave and gift. Make sure to handwrite and mail your note on nice stationery and mail it to the recipient.

Here are some wording suggestions for your 'thank you' notes

Group gift from your co-workers:

"Dear Friends, How kind of you to grace us with the gift of beautiful china dinnerware. We were so grateful to have full place settings for eight. We hope our home will be a welcoming place to invite our friends often. We look forward to having each of you for dinner in the future. Your gift will definitely be a part of many of our memory making moments. Sincerely, Mr. and Mrs. Bernard Tyler"

Monetary gift:

"Dear Uncle and Aunt Warbucks, Thank you for showing such generosity during our wedding. Just as you chose to make and investment in our future, Melvin and I chose to make several investments with the funds we received from you. We look forward to

seeing you again soon and thank you so much for traveling so far to be with us on our special day. We appreciate you both very much. With Love, Marlene (for us both)"

Every gift should be acknowledged with at thank you note. Remember that even the gifts you didn't quite like deserve thanks. Don't forget that gifts received before the wedding may be recognized immediately; you don't have to wait until after the ceremony. Be sure to get yours in the mail as soon as you return from your honeymoon and no later than 3-4 weeks after the wedding.

Wedding Shower Thank You Notes

It is a common and necessary courtesy to thank those who have showered you with gifts during your wedding shower. Take the time to leave a gracious and heartfelt impression on these guests by composing and sending out thank you cards that show just how appreciative you are of their time and money.

Here are some tips to help with your shower gift thank you cards.

The hostess/host should definitely receive both a card and perhaps even a thank you gift. Be sure to point out how grateful you are and how much you enjoyed the shower. A nice gift certificate to a movie or dinner would be a nice gesture of thanks as well.

Take the time to hand write your cards. Handwritten cards are more personal and they show the recipient that you took the time and effort to pen a card for especially for him or her. Your card should include specific language that mentions their gift and how you will use or enjoy it in the future. Try to **have these completed and mailed within two weeks** after the shower.

A great tip is to practice your notes on a separate piece of paper and then transfer the finished sentiment, in black ink, onto special 'Thank You' stationery with matching envelopes. Add a seal for a unique touch.

Use a genuine and personal salutation to close your thanks. Two appropriate ones include: *Very Sincerely Yours*, and *With Heartfelt Thanks*.

Mail your cards preferably directly from the post office. Try to avoid hand-delivering or emailing your cards.

Thanking your family and friends quickly and appropriately is very important. Remember that they have taken the time to shower you with love and friendship--not to mention a gift, just because they love and care about you. Make sure you show your gratitude for their efforts.

Spa Etiquette

If you and your bridesmaids or groomsmen are planning a trip to a day spa in preparation for the big day, you should probably brush up on your spa etiquette before you go. **Listed here are some everyday tips to help you spa well at home and abroad**

> **Always see to your personal hygiene** before your visit. This includes making sure you have fresh breath. Don't drink alcohol before your appointment; not only is this dehydrating but it could be quite unpleasant for your therapist!

> **Try not to drink or eat too much before your appointment** Eating before you go will cause your blood flow to concentrate in your stomach area. Likewise drinking a lot of fluid will cause you to have to go to the bathroom which will interrupt your treatment.

> **Leave your jewelry in your safe.** Not only do most treatments require that you take off your clothing, but you'll also have to remove your jewelry. You don't want to chance leaving expensive or sentimental jewels behind so to be safe try not to wear any to your appointment.

> **The International Spa Association recommends** that you shower before your appointment. This shows respect for your therapist and will enable you to more readily relax. Another tip: try a sauna before your massage or treatment.

> **Be honest** with your therapist and let him or her know immediately if the music choice bothers you or if it is just too loud. If it is too cold or too hot, let them know that too.

Relax. Enjoy this time of pampering so that you will get the most for your dollar. Massage has many benefits and is growing in popularity more every day.

Remember that in many foreign countries (to the United States of America) the culture is more laid back about subjects like nudity. If you are concerned about whether you will be asked to disrobe at your appointment do some research and check ahead about local customs and mores. If you know that you are not willing to get naked for the treatment you may want to pass on the experience or try a facial or pedicure instead. Whatever you decide don't let this become a matter of anxiety or stress during your vacation time; it simply isn't worth it. Go visit a great museum instead.

to respond to local customs and traditions regarding spas while traveling abroad.

Bridesmaid Etiquette

My Role and Duties for her Big Day

What is a Bridesmaid?

In the traditional wedding ceremony, the bride is usually attended by young ladies of marriageable age. These attendants are referred to as *Bridesmaids*. The chief, or lead, bridesmaid is called the *Maid-of-Honor* if she is unwed and the *Matron-of-Honor* if she is married. Younger girls who are obviously too young to be married may also be included and are called *Junior Bridesmaids*.

Why was I asked to participate and what is my role?

The Bridesmaid tradition is thought to have originated in Bible times during the ceremonies of Jacob, Leah and Rachel. Each of these sisters brought their own attendants or servants to the wedding and these were to serve from that point forward as their personal handmaidens. Another popular thought in the West attributes the bridesmaid tradition to an ancient Roman law, which required that there be at least ten witnesses at a wedding in order to outsmart any evil spirits in attendance. It was believed that the attendants, by dressing in identical clothing to the bride and groom, would confuse the spirits so that they would not know who to curse.

Basically the Bridesmaid is someone who is dear to the couple and she is called upon to offer **emotional support** on perhaps the biggest day of a young lady's life. Other duties may include doing things like **helping the bride choose her bridal ensemble, addressing envelopes, hosting the bridal shower or bachelorette party and standing up with her on the wedding day**.

Special honor may be given to the **Maid or Matron of Honor** before and during the service. She **may be asked to help the bride dress, hold her flowers during the ceremony, assist her with her veil during the ceremony or arrange her train once she is at the altar.** Most Maids or Matrons of Honor are also asked to serve as a witness by signing the marriage license and holding the groom's wedding band. In addition, she and the Best Man will probably be asked to propose a toast during a formal Reception. The Junior-Bridesmaid is only responsible to show up to the wedding and look adorable.

What will my costs include?

There was a time when the bride's family covered all or most of the wedding expenses. This is still the case in some cultures and on some rare occasions here in America. However, most modern day bridesmaids are expected to cover their own expenses. These costs might include any or all of the following.

> **Bridesmaid Ensemble.** This includes your shoes, dress and jewelry. Most brides cover the cost of their bridesmaid's flowers.

> **Travel Expenses.** This would include your travel to and from the wedding location as well as your accommodations once you have arrived.

> **Bridal Shower.** Together with the other maids, most bridesmaids choose to host either a bridal party, tea or shower in honor of their bride.

Use this information to make an informed decision. Should you decide to be a bridesmaid, make sure you are an asset to the party as this is a very exciting yet stressful time in your friend's life. Do your best to meet deadlines, plan ahead for known expenses, have your fittings done when asked, make sure you have the agreed upon shoes and jewelry and get a fresh and pretty hairstyle for the big day. If you don't think you can afford to be a bridesmaid be honest and let your bride-to-be know as soon as possible. If you cannot serve, make a point to offer your assistance in some other way and be sure to come and support your friend on her big day. Have fun!

Daytime Wedding Dress for Guests

Of all of the celebrations of life I think I'd have to say my favorite public one is a beautiful romantic wedding. Everyone tries to do their very best when it comes to weddings. In general if you are attending a church wedding there is an automatic formality to the service versus a wedding on the beach in Bermuda. At either wedding I think these tips will be helpful when you are deciding what to wear.

For the daytime wedding think business attire. Ladies, this is the time to wear a nice pastel or colorful dress or suit. Gentlemen, you can wear your suit with a bright tie and perhaps a great color-coordinated shirt in a dusty pink or blue. Put your best foot forward, figuratively and literally. Don't forget the shoes.

When you are dressing for weddings remember these tips:

The Bride Wears White. Call me old-fashioned but it is still considered the bride's day to shine. Let her wear white while you opt for another fabulous color.

Complete The Look. Basically, unless you are on the beach you should dress in an appropriately dressed-up way. Ladies, this is the day you can wear your hat or a nice scarf and brooch. Also, wear nylons (hosiery) they really do lend an air of class and style. Gentlemen, shine your shoes and wear a tie with a matching handkerchief. You'll look really smart.

Bring your Smile. Like Little Orphan Annie always says, you're never fully dressed without a smile. Attend the wedding with a winning attitude and prepared to have a great time. Choose to either leave your hang-ups (about the couple) at home or graciously decline the invitation. This is neither the time nor place to make a statement.

One more note, if you have not been able to send your wedding gift ahead, be sure to ask the host or hostess where they are placing the gifts. You don't want to walk into the ceremony with the gift; someone may think it's a new style of handbag. Have a great time; I am sure you'll look fabulous.

Wedding Gift Etiquette

Standards for Wedding Gift Giving

Send your gift ahead it is beneficial to shop early and send your gift ahead of the actual wedding date. This tends to be a custom that varies by region. For instance, people on the **East Coast** usually prefer to send their gift ahead of time or soon after the actual wedding. It is not recommended that you bring gifts to the ceremony. This will cause the couple to have to transport gifts on their special night. In the **Midwest** it is considered acceptable for the couple to set up a gift table at the reception where the guests can place their gifts.

Gifting money or gift certificates is perfectly fine and many couples even set up 'Wishing Well' tables or an alternative in order to receive monetary gifts. These you should take with you to the reception where it can be presented directly to the couple. If you have decided to give the couple money in lieu of a gift, you should give only what you can afford. Some people have set unrealistic guidelines which state that you should give a certain amount to the bride and groom per person in order to offset their costs. This is not true. As a wedding guest you have no obligation whatsoever to pay for any portion of the wedding celebration. The only reason you should be invited is because you are dear to the couple and they want you to be a witness to their joyous event.

If you are sending a gift prior to the wedding you should send it either to the home of the bride's parents or to the return address on the invitation. Although, social etiquette rules state that you have up to one year after the wedding to send a gift, this really should be done as soon as possible after you receive your invitation. You should send a wedding gift whether you are able to attend the ceremony or not. The exception is if you have not been in contact with the couple for an extended time and/or you don't live in close proximity. In these cases you are under no obligation to send a gift, although a card or note of congratulations would be thoughtful.

Chalk it up as an oversight or tackiness if you do not receive a thank you note for your gift within a couple of months. I would not recommend contacting the couple; however, it is acceptable to contact the bride or groom to find out if the gift was received in instances when you have mailed. Otherwise, realize it is tacky to discuss or bring up the gift.

Gift-giving should be an enjoyable experience. You should not have to be stressed or worried in any way as you shop. I hope these wedding gift etiquette guidelines have helped you to understand that the key thing for you as a guest is to give from the heart and join the couple as they celebrate a great and memorable day in their new lives together.

Funeral Etiquette

If you are attending a funeral it is probably safe to say that you have lost either a family member, close friend or someone whom you respected and want to pay a final homage to like a business associate or boss. As a general rule, most people do not attend the funerals of strangers that said you should not have to feel uncomfortable about going to the service since you will most likely be among people you know. Notwithstanding the relationship, if you have decided to attend a service, the traditional funeral should be pretty straightforward and easy to follow. Be aware however that many families are choosing to personalize the services for their deceased loved one and so it is important to follow their lead during the ceremony.

Most funeral services tend to be somewhat solemn, but there is an increasing trend toward a more celebratory mood during funerals. However, regardless of the mood, there are some etiquette requirements that you should always observe every time.

Funeral Etiquette

Arrive early. You should always endeavor to arrive at the church or funeral home at between 15 to 20 minutes before the service is scheduled to begin. Take your seat quietly, and reverently await the arrival of the family. Try to sit somewhere in the middle to back of the sanctuary or hall. The first few rows are generally reserved for the family and close friends of the deceased. If the decedent is presented and the casket is open you may take this time to take a last look at him or her. If you arrive late, enter quietly, taking your place on the back row. Your goal should be to draw as little attention to yourself as possible, making every effort not to disrupt the service.

Think conservative. Funerals tend to be solemn events. Take care to dress and behave in a conservative manner that reflects your respect for the deceased. Conservative dress might include business wear or a simple dress. This is not the time for 'party' type dresses. Men should dress in a suit with a classic tie.

Participate. The funeral will most likely be conducted by a clergy member or designated speaker. You should feel free to join in during the ceremony. This would include standing during prayers and singing during any congregational or group singing. Even if you are not religious it is customary to stand or bow during the prayer time as a show of recognition for their tradition.

Follow the lead of those leading the ceremony. If you aren't clear as to whether or not you should join or participate simply remain solemn and quiet.

Follow the order of dismissal. During most funeral processions the family will follow the casket out of the church or funeral home. Very often the attendees are then dismissed using an orderly row by row method. Leave the building promptly, following the prescribed order and make sure not to hold up the flow of the dismissal. If you are planning to attend the graveside ceremony you should get to your car quickly and wait for the traffic directors to summons you. Make sure that you turn your headlights on so that you are identified to other drivers as part of the procession.

One other matter you may want to consider about attending funerals deals with whether or not children should attend. Funeral services tend to be very emotion-filled experiences. Therefore, it is not normally recommended that you take along very young children unless they are intimately related to the deceased. Even then you may want to consider whether they should go or not. Should you choose to allow your children to attend make sure that you prepare them for what will be happening during the services. If you know that the body will be displayed you will want to discuss this with them as well. If this is their first funeral you will definitely want to take a seat toward the back of the venue.

If Mary's Dog Dies Send Her a Note of Condolences

There are very few instances in life that are not spoken to by the rules of what is commonly called etiquette. For decades now we have seen a steady decline in the practice and teaching of such social graces as manners and etiquette however, these are both still very necessary to polite society. When rules of etiquette are ignored it never fails that someone winds up finding themselves in an awkward situation feeling uncomfortable.

The practice of etiquette derives from the desire by an individual or group to put another's comfort above their own. A very key concept to be grasped and acted upon when seeking to prove adept at being gracious deals with the idea of being considerate of others and seeking their good and comfort. The person of civility will always exhibit cultured behavior toward others.

Funerals tend to be a time of anxiety and tension. During this time many people have questions about how they are expected to behave before, during and after the death of a loved one. Just exactly what do the rules of etiquette have to say about correct behavior or social etiquette in times of grief? There are definitely some social *yays* and *nays* that should be adhered to and practiced in order that the deceased is not defamed. In addition, every effort should be made not to embarrass the family of the deceased due to a lack of, what might be perceived as, class.

Considering basic rules of etiquette to be followed after the loss of a loved one here are some basic guidelines to follow.

In general the close relatives of the deceased ought not to be seen socially at parties and large events immediately after their loss. For instance, **wedding and party invitations may be declined during this time** and no one should fault the family for their absence.

It is important and shows kindness to **acknowledge the death of a close friend or family member** through any of several methods. To show your condolences you might send a note or visit the family. Certainly gifts of flowers and food are both appropriate to send or take to the grieving family and if you are prevented from attending the funeral (due to distance or illness) a note should definitely be sent explaining your absence.

If you are a member of the mourning family you will want to **appoint someone or several people to make sure that "Thank You" notes are sent** out as soon as possible to anyone who showed any kindness during your family's time of mourning. The family should be sure to word any requests for donations to a charity or the like as one coming from them and not the deceased. These would then read something along the lines of, "The family of Roger Smith requests that …."

Finally, when dealing with what to do or what not to do it is always a good policy to err on the side of conservativeness in your behavior. **If you are not certain whether you should do something or not either research accepted behavior or just don't do it.**

Funeral Attendance Etiquette

Question: Should I attend my ex mother-in-law's funeral?

In most instances the answer to the question of whether or not to attend someone's funeral is pretty clear in one's heart. **If you have to ask, and are feeling the nudge to go you probably ought to attend.** We normally attend a funeral out of respect and honor for the deceased. Consider the message you might be sending to your former family members, children and perhaps grandchildren if they perceive you have snubbed their beloved 'Nana.'

In some cases, where there has been a bitter and nasty divorce you may want to reconsider attending an in-law's funeral service. Despite your feelings about your former spouse, **if your mother or father–in-law was always kind and inclusive toward you, it would be rude not to attend the service.** Still, you should consider whether your presence will cause discomfort or confusion during an already very emotional time. If you believe your being there will cause extra anxiety or frustration to the situation **choose instead to send a heartfelt card along with an appropriate floral arrangement to the family .**

Consider your children. If you have children together with your ex and they are going to attend inquire as to whether they would like for you to accompany them. Their needs should outweigh any personal vendettas or agendas for both sides.

Remember if you do decide to attend that you may have a different role than you would, had you still been the daughter or son-in-law. If your former spouse is still unmarried this may not cause much disturbance at all. However, **take your cues from the grieving family.** Although you may feel that you are still one of them, they may not have the same opinion. **Offer your help and be gracious** during the service and if there are hard feelings you may want to bow out gracefully immediately after. You should probably not expect to ride in the limousine during the procession. However, if your children need your support and comfort during the ride, show the courage and fortitude necessary to accompany them without apology. **In your children the two families became one; their emotional needs trump attitudes and even preferences during this stressful time.**

What Should I Write In A Letter To An Acquaintance Who Just Lost Her Husband?

Question: What Should I Write In A Letter To An Acquaintance Who Just Lost Her Husband?

Letters of sympathy are probably the most difficult to pen. It is a little easier to write a condolence if you are able to draw upon the experience and memories relative to your own losses. Still anyone is capable of writing a sincere and thoughtful note that uses tact and exudes understanding and empathy.

Answer:

Sample note on the **Death of Husband or Wife**

My dear Mrs. Kimball,

I was very sorry to learn the sad news about your husband's passing. I hope with this note to offer my sincerest sympathy at this time.

Although I did not know Mr. Kimball well, his reputation was such that I can only imagine how much he will be missed and mourned by both your family and our community for which he worked so tirelessly during his lifetime. Very sincerely yours, Mrs. Mary Riley

What Do I Wear To A Funeral?

When dressing for a funeral you should always choose something that is conservative. Your clothing choice should reflect your respect and recognition that this is a solemn occasion in honor of a friend or loved one.

Here are some general tips to assist you in choosing the appropriate dress for attendance at a funeral or graveside service.

Women.

> **Choose black.** I don't think you can ever go wrong with a black dress or suit. These wardrobe items are both very versatile. In addition, either of these options is easily suited for both dressy to

conservative wear. This makes either choice appropriate dress for many occasions. Choosing a black dress or suit will send the message that you are reverent and honoring of the deceased. This is definitely not a time for you to wear loud or splashy colors. If you don't want to wear black, other great color options include navy blue and grey.

Think conservative. Funerals tend to be solemn events. Take care to dress and behave in a conservative manner that reflects a reverent attitude. Conservative dress might include a nice business suit or a simple dress. Take care to cover your shoulders and knees. Pass on the cocktail party look and opt for a more sedate appearance.

Wear a hat This is a perfect occasion to wear your favorite hat. Hats give a polished look and will complete your ensemble in a classic yet stylish way. Keep in mind your hat should not be gauche or outlandish.

Tone down the jewelry. Most stylishly elegant women will want to include their jewels, even during a funeral. Try not to appear overly adorned by sticking with one ring per hand and maybe a classic string of pearls. Again, you want to reflect a mourning spirit without sacrificing style.

Use shoe sensibility. A funeral is not the time to choose very high heels or shoes that are notoriously uncomfortable (no matter how fabulous they look). You are headed in to a high stress situation and the last things you want to worry about are your feet. Choose comfort over glamour and you will be grateful. Funerals normally involve a great deal of standing and walking, especially if you are planning to attend the graveside service.

Just in case... I always recommend carrying along a trusty umbrella and an extra handkerchief or two. My experience includes quite a few rainy funeral services so it's better to be safe (and dry) than soggy.

Men.

A conservative suit. As mentioned above, the black conservative cut black suit is a perfect choice for a funeral. Other great choices include a grey or dark blue suit. Regardless of the suit you choose you should wear a crisp white collared shirt with a nice tie. Try to avoid loud colors.

Wear a hat and a trench If you are a hat wearer feel free to wear one to the funeral. A nice fedora style is a great choice. Complete the look with a classic black or dark trench.

Tone down the jewelry. Try to avoid any jewelry other than a wedding band and a watch. Remember your goal is to show respect and reverence. You don't want to draw undo attention to yourself.

Shoe shine. Take an extra minute to shine up your dress shoes before you go. This will complete a polished and elegant look that is not distracting.

Just in case... Again, carry along an umbrella just in case it begins to rain. The extra hankies are nice just in case you need to offer a shoulder or more to an overly distraught loved one or friend..

Children.

I don't normally recommend that very young children attend funerals unless they are members of the immediate family. Still, there is certainly nothing wrong with choosing to take them along.

How to Write a Sympathy Card

Sincere Notes That Comfort

"Do not be afraid of showing your affection. Be warm and tender, thoughtful and affectionate. Men are more helped by sympathy, than by service; love is more than money, and a kind word will give more pleasure than a present." (John Lubbock, English Biologist and Politician, 1834-1913)

We must always remember that the goal and purpose behind the practice of etiquette is interacting and communicating well and comfortably with those around us. We want to do the right thing and writing a kind note of sympathy is one way to accomplish this goal when someone you know or love is hurting.

Following are some key essentials you should include in your note which will be helpful as you seek to comfort and serve.

Write From the Heart

- **Remember your goal** in writing a note of sympathy is to express your sorrow over the person's loss or illness, to comfort and to encourage. Before you set pen to paper, decide how you will word your note. In other words, practice the wording on a plain sheet of paper before writing on your actual stationery or card.
- **Please hand write** preferably using black ink which is always formal and, I believe, easier to read. A fine point black rollerball-type pen is always a great choice when writing important or sincere notes. Neatly address your envelope (also by hand) and make sure you address the recipient's family when appropriate. Here's an example: Mr. and Mrs. Thomas McMann and Family
- **Show your concern** by speaking to the situation directly. Mention the deceased by name and make sure you mention some fond memory you have of him or her. If the situation involves someone who is gravely ill or who has been injured, ask how you may be of assistance and include any means they may use to contact you.
- **Be sincere** by considering carefully any offers to assist your grieving friend. Ideally, you might offer a specific way to help-- but only if you choose to make yourself available. For instance, you may want to mention that you are available to watch a

couple's children while the surviving spouse handles any of the many tasks associated with funerals, deaths, hospitals and insurance.

- **Close well** using a sincere and heartfelt sentiment such as: "You're in our thoughts and prayers," or "With love and prayers." Think of your note as a great big loving hug of support in your absence.
- **Make yourself available** by following up in any of several ways after a few days or weeks have passed. If you are in close proximity you might even consider making a visit to check on the bereaved. If you live far away you can check in either by sending another note, making a phone call or even determining to make contact frequently by email correspondence.
- **Invest in a set of stationery.** A box of fine stationery or unique hand-made cards is always great to have on hand for use in any of the situations listed above.

A sympathy note is a necessary, loving and meaningful way for friends and family to show their support when a loved one is grieving or ill. During this difficult time your note is an opportunity to encourage; it may well be the only bright spot your loved one has all day!

Technology Etiquette

Cell Phone Etiquette

When the Post family and Ann Landers were giving advice about matters of etiquette the now indispensable electronic we know as the cell phone was not a big deal. The telephones they referred to were those almost obsolete dinosaurs we now refer to as 'landlines.' However, in the year 1960, the world's first partly automatic car phone system, *Mobile System A (MTA)*, was launched in Sweden and we have been evolving into a mobile focused global society ever since. (Contributors, 2011) I am not naïve enough to suggest that you leave your cell at home or turn it off unless you need to use it but, I would like to offer that you should evaluate your dependence upon it and recognize whether or not you are behaving appropriately within your life situations. If you are not using your cell phone in a way that is considerate of others perhaps you might consider making the necessary adjustments so that you can achieve your goal of being a lady or gentleman who respects others and exhibits good manners.

The home phone was once a staple in every home but with the advent and exponential growth of the cell phone many people today view them as antiquated relics from the past. Here is a point to remember: while there are similarities between etiquette for home phones and your cell by nature the truth is that you are more likely to inconvenience others with your cell phone than with your home phone. Let's look then at polite ways to handle situations involving your (or someone else's) cell phone.

> I think it is important to **remember that your cell phone is for your convenience** and not a way for others to track you down. That said, realize that you do not have to answer your phone each time it rings. If your phone rings and you are alone and not actively involved in a conversation or another activity-of course answer your cell phone. However, if you are at a dinner party or playing a game of tennis you needn't stop to answer your phone; 99 percent of the time the call will wait.

> When answering your cell **always be polite** answering with a simple "hello" or "this is John."

When you are making a call you should **always identify yourself and give a proper greeting** to the person on the other line. Only then should you ask to speak with the person you are calling.

If you need to yell or call out loudly, excuse yourself, **place the caller on hold and then call out**.

Whenever you attend a movie or play at the theater (or visit another quiet venue such as a library) you should always **place your cell phone on vibrate or the silent mode**. Once again if it rings you may certainly check it if you think you should, but only accept the call after relocating outside of the room. It is absolutely acceptable to press "ignore" on your phone and move to a private location to return the call if necessary.

Never text or dig through your purse or another bag for your cell phone **while you are driving**. Staggering statistics from the Human Factors quarterly journal in 2005 reveal "Cell phone distraction causes 2,600 deaths and 330,000 injuries in the United States every year." The same study reported that motorists who are talking on their cell phone while driving are more incapacitated than drunk drivers with blood alcohol levels exceeding .08. Please don't use your cell phone while you are driving.

Try to refrain from talking on your cell while you are driving. The driver who is talking on his or her cell phone is highly distracted and incapable of giving his/her full attention to the serious task of driving. In consideration of other drivers you should pull over and park in order to make cell phone calls when you are in the car.

Don't accept calls on your cell phone when you are having a face to face conversation with someone. It is the height of rudeness to interrupt a conversation-regardless of the situation-in order to answer your cell phone. If you absolutely must take the call (if you have been awaiting an important call for instance) you should conclude your conversation and with an apology step away to somewhere private and return the call.

Don't use loud or offensive ringtones on your cell. This could prove embarrassing to you and others dependent upon the situation. Remember that others will identify you by the choices you make and your ringtone is definitely a choice.

The cell phone is a wonderful and needful tool. Today's smartphones enable us to literally have the world at our fingertips at all times. Enjoy this advancement as it has definitely made for an improved life in many ways. I love my phone and am at a loss when I think about how I ever got along as well without it. The cell phone is a great tool. Remember then that it is always the abnormal use or abuse of a matter, thing or situation that makes it objectionable. Always use your cell phone using respect and courtesy toward others and you will be noted as a person who is considerate, kind, classy and admirable.

What Do I Do When My Cell Rings During Dinner

Question: What Do I Do When My Cell Rings During Dinner

My friends like to stay in touch and sometimes even my employer calls me at odd times. Should I answer my phone while I am at dinner?

Answer:

The cell phone has become a necessity. I love mine and I appreciate that it is a great tool. However, there is a time and place for cell phone conversations.

If you are dining, whether it be at home, at a friend's home or at a restaurant, you should definitely turn off your cell phone. If you are unwilling to turn it off, it should at least be put on silent mode.

Answering and holding a conversation during dinner or at the dining table is considered rude behavior. The message you send by talking on the phone during dinner is that this call or person calling is more important to you than those with whom you are dining. If you are dining alone feel free to hold a conversation. Still, if you are eating it may cause discomfort to the person with whom you are speaking. It really is okay to be out of pocket for a moment. Take a little time off and just relax and enjoy your meal with family and/or friends uninterrupted.

Handling Cell Phone Interruptions

When you are out and about, perhaps at a department store or even at your favorite ice cream parlor, there is no guarantee that your cell phone won't ring. This is perfectly understandable, after all your friends and family don't know when and where you are at all times. In most instances however, you have simply crossed their mind and now they want to call and touch base or ask you a quick question. These are all normal, everyday situations that are easily handled graciously. The key is to understand that the cell phone is a handy tool that aids in the quality of life. Each ring does not constitute an emergency so calm down and answer when you become available.

Statistics from the year 2010, report that the wireless revenues from the cell or wireless industry were a whopping 159.9 billion dollars. (U.S. Wireless Quick Facts). Based on these statistics, one can assess the fact that there are a lot of people in our country who use their cell phones quite a bit during the day.In fact, 26.6 percent of all American households are only wireless, meaning that they have no tradition or 'landline' phone at all. With all of these cell phones out there, we are all candidates for at least one daily cell phone encounter.

Here are some helpful tips for handling cell phone interruptions when you are in public or unavailable to answer.

Use your caller id information. This information really does have a purpose. Screening is a helpful process that allows you to be able to assess the nature of a call with a glance. Executives and managers have utilized their personal administrative assistants to handle call-screening for them for many years. Think of your caller id screen as your own personal assistant. The phone rings and the screen announces, *"Pardon me Mrs. Kimbley, but there is a Mr. Charles Frazier on line one for you."*

Be wise about your ringtone. Take care that you choose a ring tone that really reflects who you are and what you believe. Whether it seems fair or not, people will make determinations about who you are based on the music that you have chosen on your cell phone. It sounds crazy, but it is true. Even your cell phone is sending a message about your values, personality and style. Try to choose something that is truly as unique as you.

Adjust your ringer volume. When you are in public you should make sure that your phone's ring tone volume is low enough that it is not startlingly loud and obtrusive to others around you. Silencing the phone is actually a great option as long as you have a vibrate setting. Use the vibration setting to alert you of incoming calls. Again, with a glance you can know whether this is an important call that you need to return immediately.

Excuse yourself. If you have determined that the incoming call is important, excuse yourself from the presence of others as quickly as possible and receive the call in private. If you fear missing the call you can always answer, mute, excuse yourself and then take the call. At any rate you should recognize that talking loudly on the phone in public is considered rude and sometimes even obnoxious behavior.

We live in a technology driven era where cell phones are as plentiful as are cars. While we all love and appreciate the instant availability of the tool, we must take the time and effort necessary to make sure our use of them is both courteous and wise.

It is true to say that the cell phone has revolutionized the way the world communicates. However, you should be aware that it has also revolutionized the spread of germs and disease. Armed with this information use you may prevent yourself and someone else from spreading harmful bacteria and viral illnesses.

Dr. Charles Gerba, a professor of environmental biology at the University of Arizona, has conducted numerous germ studies in pursuit of greater information on the spread of disease through cell phones. He has determined that cell phones are among the dirtiest surfaces we touch every day, even dirtier than a toilet seat. Consider The germ counts found during a recent study of cells at offices in major U.S. cities such as Los Angeles, Washington DC, San Francisco and New York. This study showed that the average cell phone contains 25,127 germs per square inch. Compare that to desktops which contained around 20,961 germs per square inch or toilet seats with 49 germs per square inch.

Dr. Gerba, who is often referred to as 'Dr. Germ' has revealed that he **once tested 25 mobile phones and found staph bacteria growing on fifty percent of them.** The staph bug can cause skin infections and meningitis, among other maladies.

Considering the statistics the wise man or woman should take pains to protect themselves and others from the spread of harmful germs. This is easy to do and simply requires responsible use. In short, **you should not**

borrow another person's cell phone and neither should you allow anyone to use yours. Although we may not think about it much, cell phones are actually quite personal. The cell is in constant contact with your hands, face and mouth which are all highly susceptible to the transmission of germs. In addition, when your cell is not in use, it is generally stored somewhere closed and warm like a pocket or a purse. Because of the warmth and potential moisture, these are both great breeding areas for any germs and bacteria that has found its way to your phone.

In order to stay off the spread of disease here are some everyday tips to follow.

Wash your hands frequently.

It is a great idea to make a habit of periodically washing your hands. The hands touch so much throughout the day and pick up so many germs. Keeping clean hands, washed with hot soapy water, is a great first step to maintaining cell phone health.

Keep your phone clean.

There are products on the market for cleaning your phone, but all you really need is a good old fashioned alcohol wipe. Use one periodically throughout the day to kill germs. This really works.

Regard your phone as a personal item.

Sure, your children and spouse will play on your phone--especially if it is a smartphone/android type. But, besides them you should really keep it to yourself. It may seem difficult to tell someone 'no' if you are asked to use your phone. Keep in mind that your phone is personal. You keep it in your purse or pocket, you put it to your face throughout the day and you carry it into your home. With that in mind, hopefully you can find a way to let the person know that you are not comfortable with him or her using your cell. Perhaps you can even just let them know that this is a predetermined policy you have and that you never allow others to use your cell phone. Think of it as a comb or tooth brush, you would never let another use either of these.

In case of an emergency, be a good neighbor.

This advice to not share your phone is intended to speak to everyday

50

situations and circumstances. In the case of an emergency you may want to consider either dialing for the other person, allowing them to use your phone with headphones or the speaker or just allowing them to use the phone themselves. Remember, if you can keep your phone sanitized this won't be a major deal and you should be perfectly fine. Rise to the occasion and be there when you are needed.

Etiquette rules are never meant to be restrictive, but rather they are encouraged in order to help you as a person live and communicate better within your community. Rules and expectations enable us to better understand what is expected from us and others as we interact inter-personally every day.

Email Etiquette Tips

Email has become the easiest and fastest way to communicate both personally and in business. This has become such a phenomena that the ever trusty United States Postal Service is struggling to find ways to stay in business.

I suppose it is no surprise to anyone that Email etiquette, often referred to as *Netiquette,* is a hot topic for today's culture. There are many reasons for this increased interest in email etiquette. Emails are sent every day by a broad section of the American population. Nearly every household has at least one computer with internet access and within those households are moms, dads, children, teens and maybe even grandparents and all or most of these are receiving and sending emails.

Consider this, Hotmail, Microsoft's industry leader in email service boasts between 350-375 million active email account users in late 2010. Yahoo! mail reported having provided close to 275 million email user accounts (2011). Knowing this you can see why it is so important that you understand how to write well and with courtesy even when you are communicating by email. Although we live in a microwave, internet driven epoch and no one wants to take the time to write a long-hand letter even though it is so much more intimate and personal.

Nevertheless, there are many circumstances in which the email is a perfect alternative to 'snail' mail. Here are some tips to help you communicate effectively and professionally when you are engaged in email conversations either at work or at home.

Prepare. Before you begin typing an email, whether it is an initial note or a response, you should ask yourself what it is that you would like to communicate through this email. In short, what is your purpose for writing? Once you know, you can read over the completed mail, before sending it out, to make sure you have accomplished your goal. If it makes the grade, then send it; if the text is confusing or unclear then perhaps you should begin again.

Communicate. Remember that you are communicating with a real person who will receive this mail from you. With that in mind you should make sure to address the person by name and be respectful. Communication involves listening, speaking and understanding. If this is a response to a received email you should take the time to address any questions or requests within the note.

Breathe. We have all been guilty at some point or another of losing our composure. If you receive an email that angers or upsets you, do not respond in kind. Take the high road and either respond only to acknowledge receipt or take some time before responding so that you can calm down and respond thoughtfully. You never want to respond to an email (or any other form of communication) in anger. When we are angry we tend to say (or write) things that we either don't mean or don't need to say. Remember that once your email gets sent it is out there forever.

Be Transparent. Your subject line should be a true representation of why you are contacting the recipient. Use phrases that relate to the subject of the mail. This is true whether you are composing a business or personal email. For instance, if you are writing an email to your mom about her visit next week, your subject line should read something like, *"Your visit."*

Research. If you are sending an email to a business associate or someone similar it is appropriate for you to use his or her last name and title. You should be careful to do the research and address the recipient correctly. The president of the company could either be addressed as Mr. Taylor or President Taylor.

Spell Check. The use of spell check is important when you are communicating in writing. When you send a note full of errors it communicates that you are sloppy or that you do not pay attention to detail. Try to always run the spelling check or use a program that auto-corrects.

Proof. You should take the extra few seconds or minutes that are necessary in order to do a quick proofread of any email you plan to send. Take this time to edit any awkward sentences or to place any missing punctuation marks.

Tone. Sometimes an email may come off incorrectly. The tone of your email is very important. Because this is written communication you should make sure that your tone is pleasant and that it is a true representation of what you wanted to say. Remember that your recipient can't hear the chuckle in your voice, neither can they see the smile on your face. Unless you want to preface everything your write you should avoid any language in the email that may be misconstrued in any way.

Brevity. Try not to write a novel when you email. Most people really do not want to read that much in an email. If the email is necessarily lengthy, try to help the recipient out by highlighting key points or summarizing the subject in the opening paragraph.

Communicate Well. The last thing you want to do in your email is confuse the reader. Take the time to be clear and concise in your writing.

Even when sending e-mail correspondences don't forget these important tips:

Use proper language mechanics

When you are answering or initiating an email, try to be courteous and appropriate in your writing. Remember that it is hard to know when someone is joking or not when one is reading so it is best to keep it straight. Try to spell words out and not use cutesy acronyms like 'Lol.'

Emails are private

You should never read an email that is not addressed to you directly, unless you are invited to by the recipient. If you approach a computer screen or see a printed copy and it is not directed to you simply step or way or avoid reading the contents.

The web is forever

Think before you send an email. In most instances, you will not be able to recall the mail so you want to make sure you say what you meant to say. This is not the best method of having personal conversations that involve intimate details and the like.

Watch your capitalization.

When typing emails, all capital writing is considered yelling over the web, so you should try not to use all caps. In addition, although it seems harmless (and a great way to show excitement) some people may misunderstand the use of the exclamation mark. Try not to over use it in your writing.

Use the BCC, for blind copying

If you are sending out a mass mailing or to a large distribution list you should use the 'BCC' category. This is especially courteous if the recipients do not know each other and might be upset that you are sharing their email addresses with strangers. In the office with team or group emails, listing the individual email addresses in the 'CC' category is perfectly acceptable.

Respond promptly

You should make every effort to respond quickly to any email correspondence you receive. It is the polite thing to do. If you need more time to consider or investigate a matter, a simple reply stating as much will be fine. This is just a relationship courtesy you want to offer.

Address and list a subject

When you are composing an email be sure to address the recipient by name at the opening of the letter. Another thoughtful tip is to make sure you list a subject in the mail. This is so helpful to the recipient.

These tips are helpful in your everyday email correspondence. Try to remember that you are still communicating and you want to do so with style.

Business Etiquette

Self-Promotion: The Etiquette and Purpose

Most people who are working hard at what they consider self-promotion are actually promoting a product. This is a very necessary pursuit for many reasons. The most obvious reason for this type of promotion is for your business, product or brand's success. A business has got to be promoted and marketed. If you have a service, product, or something similar you have no choice but to engage in promotion.

On the other hand, very often we are bombarded by everyday people who just want to be heard from and recognized for being. There is an old saying that cream always rises to the top (the reference is to the cream in milk which is then used to make butter). This principle drives home the point that when a person does their very best, at whatever they put their mind and hand to, they will excel. Not only that people will notice their work ethic and reward them for it. The key is not blowing one's own horn but, being the real thing. Believe me if you are authentic and sincere, people will notice both and you will have the respect, esteem and acknowledgement you deserve. Let's look at the process of self-promotion. What exactly is involved and how do we do it correctly and with style.

They are called promoters for a reason. Even if this is your wife, husband, mother or father, you should try to enlist someone other than yourself to be the mouthpiece behind your promotion. It always adds credibility when you can be recommended to others. For instance a mom who meets someone who needs a florist might say: *"My daughter is a great floral designer you should look into hiring her for your wedding."* The daughter on the other hand would have to say something like this: "I am a great designer, with lots of experience. Why don't you hire me for your wedding?" Do you see the contrast? You do have another more savvy option available if you are prepared. Consider how you could also approach the subject diplomatically and without the awkwardness of having to sell your services. By having your portfolio on hand, you could graciously offer to show the bride your work and let it speak for itself. In this situation you would say something along these lines: "My name is Lara Friedman and I am a Floral Designer. I happen to have my portfolio in my car and it showcases some of my favorite wedding designs. If you have a minute I'd love to share them with you." Before leaving you should then say: "If I may, I will leave my card and brochure with you. Please feel free to call me if you have any questions about my fees, services or anything else."

Marketing Etiquette tips you could:

Rent space at a wedding (or funeral) trade fair. If you do choose this option, make sure you display professional signage that offers an accurate representation of what you have to offer. In this venue you will be dealing with an audience who are looking for what you have to offer. You can now promote your service in a friendly atmosphere while at the same time networking, distributing your business literature and gaining much needed exposure.

Market according to your style. If someone inquires or the opportunity presents itself for you to be able to showcase your product or service you must take it. Customers and clients want to know that you believe in your brand. Be confident and promote your brand effectively and with style.

Confidence Trumps Boasting. If your product/service is everything your advertisements and promotional items say, then you're not boasting you're confident. Clients like confidence. Americans want the very best of everything; if your product is the best available, have literature available that includes quotes from former clients and always have an updated list of references. Do what is needed, and ethical, to secure one more customer whenever you can.

Outsource. Sometimes we are simply too close to the project to be objective enough to do what is best for our business. This is one of the areas you will need to spend the money to get good marketing resources. It is probably best to have someone else write your press release, design your website, and at the very least proof your business cards. This is important because they will present you or your product in a way that you cannot or will not. When a professional writes that you are an expert in the field of Cosmetology with over twenty-years of experience people will assume your PR person and not you made that assertion. Followed up with a few testimonials your case will be made and you can feel confident distributing the materials knowing that your campaign was created by another. They will have a different perspective. Make sure they have enough information and then let them go to work. You will be surprised at how your marketing vision comes to life in the hands of another.

Introduction Etiquette

Making introductions can be a cause of great distress for some people because they may worry that their introduction might be handled incorrectly. Here are some helpful tips that, if followed, should aid you in making introductions in most any situation.

Introducing one person to another

Age before beauty. Remember that when making introductions the younger of the two or more being introduced should be introduced to the elder. Using the elder's name first you might say something along these lines: *"Mr. Riley, this is my friend Louise."* or *"Grandmother, I would like for you to meet my favorite teacher Mrs. Daggs."* **What if you don't know who is older?** This is a common (and good) question. If you don't know who is older and are unable to determine the truth by observation you should definitely not ask either of them his or her age. Just make a guess and introduce them using the same formula as above.

Speak clearly using good diction. Whenever you are making an introduction you should be confident and clear in your speech. Use an adult's title and last name when and if you know it. For instance, you would make the following introduction in a meeting of your mother and your baseball coach. *"Mom, this is my baseball coach, Mr. Herman."* You might even want to add a bit of extra descriptive information that will help people make the connection. In the scenario above you might add: *"He is the one I told you about who gave me his signed Babe Ruth baseball."* This will also enable them to have a talking point between them that is independent of your introduction. This principle applies to business introductions as well. Introduce your unemployed brother to the accounting manager at your dinner party adding a little extra information so that they might strike up a potentially beneficial conversation.

Introduce anyway. There will undoubtedly be times when you are in the uncomfortable predicament of having to introduce someone whose name you have forgotten. In this case you should first re-introduce yourself and then your acquaintance. This introduction should go something like this: *"I am sorry; I know that we met last year at the New Year's Eve ball but I can't seem to recall your name. My name is Grace and this is my sister Hazel."*

What about when I am being introduced?

When you are being introduced to another person you should follow the same rules that you would during self introductions.

Remember these basic introduction guidelines.

Whenever you are being introduced you should **stand,** or **face the person** if you are already standing.

If you are being introduced to someone who is seated, for instance and elderly person or someone in a wheelchair, you should **lean down** making yourself as level with the person as possible.

While you are being introduced you should always be sure to make **eye contact.** That means look him or her in the eye and smile. If you want to make friends, show yourself friendly.

Extend your hand and be sure to give a firm shake. This is a hand extended in friendship. In the medieval times it was difficult to know who was friend and who was foe. This was because the men were often covered in armor from head to toe. A right was extended in order to show the other person that there was no weapon in it and that this person was willing to be friendly. The gesture would then be returned and the greeting of friends would be completed.

In response to your introduction, it is appropriate to **say something simple and straightforward.** You might try: *"I am pleased to meet you Mr. Blair."*

Making a great first impression

Here are some last thoughts on how to avoid making a bad first impression. These are your takeaway don't do moves.

Don't avoid eye contact. This action communicates confusing messages. It may leave the person wondering if you are trustworthy or you might even appear weak, lacking confidence.

Return the handshake. Refusing someone's hand is rude. If you are wearing gloves, remove the one on your right hand out of respect.

Offer a firm handshake but not one that leaves the person wincing in pain. Neither should you offer a limp handshake that communicates weakness.

Making introductions is a very important part of etiquette both at home and in the business sector. Whenever you make someone's acquaintance you should take the time to do so properly so that you are remembered fondly and perhaps called upon to enjoy parties, attend functions, serve on committees or render a service. An introduction can either make or break a relationship.

Sick Etiquette

It happens to us all at some point during the year. We call them common colds, viruses, or maybe even influenza bugs. These illnesses are anything but pleasant and the last thing you will want to do if you have come down with a cold or flu is pass it on to your co-workers or family members. This may mean that you will need to stay home and isolated from others for a little while, but it is worth it if you can save them the aggravation and pain of becoming ill. I hope that in these cases you will not take on the attitude that misery loves company.

As you consider your responsibilities during your illness here are some tips for being thoughtful of others.

> **Stay home from work.** This is one of the rare instances when you really need to stay away from the workplace. Many office buildings operate on recycled air which makes matters even worse. If you are privy to have your own private office, you might be able to get away with coming in but you should still be careful to not spread your illness. This means you should keep your hands clean, refrain from sneezing into the open air, use tissue and hand sanitizer and if at all possible meet your deadline work and ask to be allowed to take the rest of the day off. Most employers will be more than willing so that they do not have to have an epidemic of flu or cold in the office.

> **Cancel appointments.** As soon as you know that you are coming down with an illness, take a survey of your calendar and obligations and see what you can reschedule. Just remember that when you are ill, you are taking your sickness with you and spreading unwanted germs. If you have an appointment with your hair stylist call immediately and let him or her know. If you bring illness into the salon your stylist and

his or her co-workers may become ill and lose income and time at work. This goes for lunch appointments, spa appointments and any other obligations that are not necessary and are easily rescheduled. You want to remember that very often those in the service industry only make income for work they actually complete. If your stylist has to stay off work for 3 days with a cold he or she simply doesn't get paid for those 3 days.

Keep your children home. As soon as you see that your child is ill, begin figuring out how to make arrangements to keep him or her home for the day. If the child is in nursery you have probably already made alternate arrangements for sick days. Remember that this is important for school-aged children as well. When your child attends school with a fever or runny nose and cough, the other children will be susceptible to whatever bug your child is carrying. They in turn will return home as carriers of this illness, give it to their family and the cycle of illness will continue. This is true for practices and other children gatherings. If you send your child to practice with a cold, be assured that even the child who doesn't like to share with others, will.

It is so important to use your manners and think of other people when you are making determinations about where to go and what to do when you are ill. Viral infections are so easily spread throughout communities and needlessly so. Consider quarantining yourself and your family during times of illness and be a part of the solution and not the problem during these cold and flu season epidemics.

Savvy Style and Etiquette

As with any etiquette topic, style is a great part of whether or not you accomplish the goal of doing it right. When you are savvy you are in the know. You have an understanding of the how and why of a particular situation. The savvy person is well informed and shrewd. This is why the man or woman of style seeks to gain more knowledge and increase his or her intelligence. The shrewd or savvy person has insight and sound judgment, both of which are especially poignant when it comes to business and politics. In combination then with style, you can see why the savvy, shrewd and stylish person is a winner at business and relationships.

Let's look more at some of Roget's thesaurus definitions of what we mean by style.

1. A distinctive way of expressing oneself: means.
2. Behavior through which one reveals one's personality: address, air, bearing, demeanor, manner, mien, presence. Archaic port.
3. The current custom: craze, fad, fashion, furor, mode, rage, trend, vogue. Informal thing. Idioms: the in thing, the last word, the latest thing. See style/good style/bad style, usual/unusual.
4. The word or words by which one is called and identified: appellation, appellative, cognomen, denomination, designation, epithet, name, nickname, tag, title. Slang handle, moniker.

Why does being savvy matter?

The person who has mastered the art of being relationally savvy is able to build relationships that encourage both personal and career growth. This is important because these people who tend to be proactive then manage their business and relationship interactions well. People tend to look up to a person who is savvy which further increases their realm and powers of influence. In addition, the relationally savvy person is supportive of others and able to use their savvy skills in order to reach out to others and increase productivity. The savvy person also tends to possess very strong social skills that further enable them to be dynamically interactive both inter-personally and on the cooperative corporate level.

How does this enhance or encourage advancement

Practicing etiquette in your business and personal affiliations will do wonders for your relationships and toward developing loyalty to your product, service or brand. **In short, it is important for the self-promoter to develop an attitude of community.** One major mistake non-savvy self-promoters often make is that they try to do it alone. This is a sure way of short-circuiting your development. The savvy person seeks and heeds great counsel. This includes seeking out others who can coach or mentor as well as asking good questions that will enhance their business and situation. **The savvy person knows that networking is imperative to success** and that reaching out beyond his or her scope of normal influence and involvement will do wonders toward increasing their bottom line and growth. So, the savvy person uses these proactive disciplines as part of their daily work ethic.

- **Don't limit your networks.** Reach out beyond your obvious involvement. Seek out advice and connections with supervisors, peers, family members, religious leaders, friends and others in senior positions of authority.

- **Identify role models.** Study and model your strategies and relationships after those you have observed to be successful and influential. Remember this might include public or historical figures as well as an elementary school teacher.
- **Reach out to others.** Even though every savvy person is not necessarily an extrovert, this is a quality that goes a long way toward aiding in your quest to self-promote. If you are not naturally extroverted, you can still use social networking outlets such as Facebook, Linkedin, Twitter or Tumblr to reach out.
- **Be in the know.** Etiquette dictates that you have it together and the savvy person will always know what they need and from where or whom. **Take stock** of your business needs and reach out to the right people.
- **Get a coach.** Even powerful business CEO's need mentors and coaches. A business coach or life coach can help you get where you want to be and beyond. Remember that coaching is about results and that is your ultimate goal for self-promotion.

Quotes from Famous People about 'Style'

- *"It is always self-defeating to pretend to the style of a generation younger than your own; it simply erases your own experience in history." - Renata Adler*

- *"Style is not neutral; it gives moral directions." - Martin Amis*

- *"The most durable thing in writing is style, and style is the most valuable investment a writer can make with his time. It pays off slowly, your agent will sneer at it, your publisher will misunderstand it, and it will take people you have never heard of to convince them by slow degrees that the writer who puts his individual mark on the way he writes will always pay off." - Raymond Chandler*

- *"A style does not go out of style as long as it adapts itself to its period. When there is an incompatibility between the style and a certain state of mind, it is never the style that triumphs." - Coco Chanel*

- *"Fashion can be bought. Style one must possess." - Edna W. Chase*

- *"Style is the dress of thoughts; and let them be ever so just, if your style is homely, coarse, and vulgar, they will appear to as much disadvantage, and be as ill received, as your person, though ever so well-proportioned, would if dressed in rags, dirt, and tatters." - Lord Chesterfield*

Handshake Etiquette

Have you ever wondered about the origin of handshakes? You might be interested to know that the very nature of the handshake was originally intended to show friendliness.

During the medieval times, when many of the men were covered in armor, the handshake was a manner of greeting used to show friendship. If one male extended an open hand to another was understood to mean an extension of friendship and the gesture would be returned. Of course the alternative would be a hand extended with an accompanying dagger or sword. Suffice it to say the handshake was a way to determine whether one was friend or foe.

Handshake Basics

The basic American handshake is very simple and most often used as a greeting between friends or new acquaintances. Here's how it is done:

1. The right hand is extended, thumb up and palm flat.
2. Grasp the other person's hand using a firm grip, palm on palm.
3. Hands are pumped two or three time in a vertical motion.
4. The grip is released.

You can definitely practice extending great handshakes with your friends and family members so that you can determine what is comfortable for you and others. Trying it out on a friend is much easier than starting out with strangers.

Handshake Types

- **The Hand Hug:** The "hand hug" is a popular type of handshake often used by politicians. This shake which involves the covering of the clenched hand shake with the left hand, communicates warmth, friendship, trust and honesty.
- **The Crusher:** This painful handshake is a favorite shake of aggressive people. This shake is said to display confidence and power. Considered the favorite of those who are overly

- **The Queen's Fingertips:** This handshake greeting is most commonly observed in male-female encounters. Usually the female presents her outstretched hand and the recipient grasps only a few digits of the right hand.
- **The Please Keep Back:** This handshake is usually extended when one of the parties is not too excited about the greeting. He or she may feel intruded upon or inconvenienced and the handshake will communicate the discomfort.

Handshakes in Culture

There are many alternatives to the everyday basic handshake. Many cultures have personalized the handshake for use within their community. Here are a few.

- The "jive shake" or "black man's shake," is associated with African-American culture. This handshake is performed by each person clutching the base of the other person's thumb and often leaning in to bump opposite shoulders. This shake is also a familiar greeting amongst men in some Native American cultures.
- Members of the Boy Scouts of America use a left hander shake, referred to as the 'scout shake.' This was a convention started by Lord Baden-Powell. Tradition states that Baden-Powell was impressed by a legend he heard while he was in West Africa. The story goes that two warring chiefs desiring peace confronted one another. One chief dropped both his weapon and his shield. Not only was his right hand empty of a weapon leaving him unable to attack, but his left hand was left empty of a shield and he was thus unable to defend against the weapons of the other.
- Those who practice the sport of fencing traditionally shake using the non-sworded hand at the conclusion of their bout.
- Many secret societies, fraternities and sororities employ secret handshakes enabling them to identify initiated brothers and sisters.
- Some cultures have a habit of shaking both hands.
- In Western culture, handshakes should be firm as weak handshakes are considered limp and cold.
- In European countries such as France and Italy, the norm is to shake hands every time you meet someone.
- In some Muslim countries (such as Turkey or the Arabic-speaking Middle East), a grip that is too firm is considered to be rude behavior.

- In China, not only are weak handshakes preferred, but the custom is to hold on for an extended time after the initial shake.
- In Turkey, the casual standard greeting is usually a kiss on the cheek twice. In some cultures the handshake may be concluded by the open palm of the hand being placed on the heart

As you greet others cross-culturally you should also remember that some religions, such as Orthodox Judaism and Islam, prohibit physical contact between men and women. In these situations follow the lead of the others around you. In general, men will exchange shakes with other men and likewise the women with other women. In place of a shake it is appropriate to give a short nod of your head.

Visiting Etiquette

How to be the perfect guest

"The good guest is almost invisible, enjoying him- or herself, communing with fellow guests, and, most of all, enjoying the generous hospitality of the hosts." - Emily Post

At Christmas there is so much joy and merriment in the atmosphere and families everywhere often get together for fun, fellowship, food and lots of gift-giving. During the holiday season most of us will play the role of the invited guest at one point or another. When you are invited to spend some time visiting a friend or relative here are some helpful tips for holiday visiting that will leave them praising your great manners and company.

Bring along a hostess gift. Unless you have been asked not to, you should take along a thoughtful hostess gift. For added effect wrap it nicely and attach a card replete with a touching or inspirational sentiment. Here's something to keep in mind. Even if you are visiting your mother, sister or best friend she or he will still appreciate a token gift of thanks. So be a thoughtful visitor and bring along a gift.

Wait for directions. Once you have arrived and have entered into the home, you should definitely wait to be directed into one room or another. A good host or hostess will always take the lead and you should be careful to follow their directions. They will be clear on where the socializing is happening and you should not wander into other 'off limits' areas without prior permission. If you need to use the restroom, you should ask for permission and directions to the more public powder room. If you have observed that the only restroom is upstairs on in a bedroom, you may want to try to wait until you go home. Don't ask your host or hostess for a tour of his or her home and refrain from doing things like opening the refrigerator or closed doors. This behavior is considered rude.

Show respect for your host and his or her home. Before you arrive make a decision on how long you will stay. Try not to be the straggler or last one out. In general, don't stay too long. Likewise, you should show due respect for your hosts home by not putting your feet up on the furniture, cleaning your shoes prior to entering the house, using a coaster for your drink and being careful not to make spills.

Wait for offers. If your visit is casual and not necessarily a dinner or cocktail event, you should wait until you are offered a drink, snack or meal rather than requesting one on your own. Your host may not intend to offer either of these and your request could cause him or her to be embarrassed or uncomfortable. If you are at your mom's or sibling's home this shouldn't be an issue. Use your judgment. If you are choking on something and no offer comes, it is perfectly fine to request, "May I have a glass of water please."

Mind your graces, P's and Q's. Minding your P's and Q's is an English expression that means one should mind his or her manners and be on his or her best behavior. When we are visiting, regardless of the occasion, we should always remember to do this. Remember to be friendly and show your engaging style. If you know in advance that you are in a bad or disagreeable mood, you might want to reschedule your visit if you are able to do so as soon as you realize your predicament. If you find that your host has already made preparations for your visit, press on and make at least a short appearance out of respect for his or her time.

Proper Casual Greeting Etiquette

If you happen to encounter an acquaintance while shopping or walking along the street, it is proper to greet them cordially and continue on your way. Don't feel pressured to invite them to lunch or stop and carry on a full conversation; however, you do want to be polite and gracious showing how much you appreciate their greeting.

Offering a greeting like *"Hi, How are you?"* will require that you stop and offer a pleasant response and then continue on your way. **Approach with a smile and extend your hand to shake.** If you are outside and your hand is gloved, use your best judgment. Ideally, it would be nice to remove the glove and shake especially if the other person isn't wearing any. **Make sure to be pleasant** and avoid saying things about the lousy day you're having. No matter what is happening in your day, **offer** this acquaintance **a kind response** such as, *"I'm well thanks and you?"*

If this is someone you would really like to spend more time with, make sure they know you would like to see them again and offer your card or make arrangements to get together at an agreed upon place on another day. Recognize how nice it was to see them again and be on your way.

Awkward Situations Etiquette

Question: What should I say if someone asks if I am expecting and I am not?

A lady or gent never asks a woman if she is pregnant. Neither should you ever ask someone if she is planning to get pregnant or why she has not. Recognize that this can be a potentially painful or embarrassing subject for everyone involved.

Answer:

This is an area that requires tact and grace. In short, I hope that no one ever asks you if you are expecting, whether your wife is expecting or if you are ever planning to have children. If this has already happened to you, I apologize for whoever posed the insensitive and probing question.

If someone does approach you with questions about your fertility or childlessness the best approach might be to **simply advise the person asking that you don't discuss your personal and private family with others.** Your response should be direct and firm without being nasty.

If you are the one who has asked this question here are some things that you should consider.

- Many couples suffer from physical maladies or other circumstances which prevent them from having children naturally.
- Still others have made the choice to not have children and don't want to have to defend their position constantly.
- One other consideration concerns overweight women. If a woman is of childbearing age and has a large abdomen she may have to answer this question repeatedly. This is not only embarrassing but hurtful.

Just remember that whether a woman is pregnant or not is a personal matter. If you are expecting or even if you are not, you should never feel pressured to answer the question as it is, by nature, a rude question. If you are thinking of asking this question, resist the urge and keep in mind that if someone you know is expecting a baby she and her husband will share the happy news how and when they choose is appropriate.

Question: What should I do when someone passes gas?

There is just something about the sound of passing gas that makes us naturally want to laugh. Within your private homes and amongst your family you will and may continue to handle these situations in your own way. Realize however that most children take their clues from the adults in their lives so you may want to set some precedents early on.

Answer:

As I always tell my children, passing gas is a normal body function. That said in American culture in particular, it is considered rude behavior in polite company.

When in the company of friends, associates or strangers it is best to ignore any obvious flatulence. This would include belching and/or burping. Most people know to say excuse me if they burp or belch loudly, but passing gas has more of a stigma and is a little trickier to navigate. If someone has passed gas and the smell is overwhelming you need not mention it or comment. If you are unable to stand the smell or feel you may embarrass the person any more than he or she already is, then excuse yourself from the room for a moment, breathe some fresh air and compose yourself.

If you are the person with gas you should try to hold it if possible until you can get to the restroom, outdoors or at least away from others. If you happen to have a slip that everyone hears you may want to say something like, "Please excuse me" or, "I apologize, It seems my stomach is upset this afternoon."

What to Do When Someone Sneezes

Question: How should I respond when someone sneezes near me?

Many people in America respond immediately by saying, "God bless you." This tradition has its origins in various ancient beliefs and myths. These beliefs range from ancient Greek culture to 14th century American superstitions. For instance, some people believe that when someone sneezes they are actually expelling a sin or an evil spirit. Still others have been taught that during a sneeze one's heart actually stops beating for a second. There are many more traditions and myths about sneezes, but the truth about them may help you formulate a ready response.

Answer:

In actuality a sneeze is the body's reaction to allergens and irritants. The actual purpose of sneezing is to expel mucus containing foreign particles or irritants and thus to cleanse the nasal cavity. Sneezing is therefore potentially harmful to those within close range of the sneeze. The average sneeze contains around 100,000 infectious airborne droplets.

When someone sneezes it is perfectly acceptable for you to turn aside in order to protect yourself from the spray. It is polite to ask if they are okay or if you may help them in any way. If you have some on hand, offer him or her a tissue or handkerchief. Afterwards, using discretion you may then want to make sure that you take preventative measures against illness yourself by washing your hands and/or face.

If you are the one who is about to sneeze **make sure you cover your mouth and nose.** Not covering your sneeze is bad manners. If you feel a sneeze building and you either don't have a tissue or handkerchief or you don't have time to grab it, you should then sneeze into your sleeve while turning away from anyone in close proximity.

Common Courtesies

Public Restroom Etiquette

If you are like most people you probably do not really like having to use public restrooms. Still, on many occasions they are necessary and who hasn't been glad to see one at some point in their life.

Listed here are some of the common problems with public restrooms along with practical tips on how to deal with them gracefully.

Remember When Using Public Restrooms...

- If you make a mess on the seat or floor please make an effort to clean up after yourself. If this is impossible, at least alert the staff so that they can tend to the problem.
- If you are having gastrointestinal problems you may want to give a 'courtesy flush' once or twice as you relieve yourself. This will help eliminate unpleasant odors and embarrassment.
- Try not to use the handicap, family or baby changing stalls unless you fall into one of those categories. These facilities are available so that people who need them will have access to them.
- Try to be thoughtful by not yelling across the restroom to others or talking on your cell phone while you are in the stall.
- Remember to wash and dry your hands after using the restroom.
- If the business, hotel or restaurant has a steward in the restroom area ,don't forget to leave a tip.

These common sense tips may be used in any setting from halls and restaurants to private homes. Just remember to take care to be commonly courteous in all you do and say--even in the public restroom.

Etiquette for Owners of Traveling Dogs

Travel Etiquette

Many more establishments, be they hotels, restaurants, stores and parks are loosening their policies about pet owners and pets. Many of these strides have been achieved due to responsible pet owners' behavior and example. If you plan to travel with your dog these are some etiquette guidelines you should follow while you are away.

In general the following should be considered regardless of where you are going.

• You should always call ahead to check with the hotel or other establishment. You would not want to get somewhere out of town with your pet and have to put him or her in a kennel because you were misinformed on the website or by a friend. call ahead just to be sure.

• If you know that your dog has behavioral problems you should not travel with him or her. Only travel with a dog that is friendly and used to being around other people, especially little children. Many dogs benefit from obedience training if this tends to be a problem.

- Whenever you are in public you should keep your dog leashed. Many people, even other pet owners, are afraid of dogs. It is also true that most hotel owners, restaurant owners, store owners, and festival coordinators require that dogs be leashed upon entry.

- Whether you are traveling or just walking your dog you should always clean up after your dog. Most parks offer receptacles specifically for waste and you can purchase a pooper scooper at any pet store.

- If you and your dog are entering a market, store, festival or something similar (especially somewhere that is an outdoor venue) you should make sure your dog has relieved himself or herself before you enter the event area.

- At hotels which do allow pets, ask the clerk for a list of expectations or for answers to specific questions such as whether your dog is allowed in the hotel lobby.

- Keep your doggy company. You should never leave your dog in the hotel room alone. Even well-behaved dogs can get into mischief, especially in a new place. In addition, he or she may scare the housekeeping staff or bark incessantly due to fear or loneliness.

- See if the hotel has a specified area for walking your dog and where they would prefer they relieve themselves. You don't want to have these odors near the doors, cars and windows.

- The restaurants that allow dogs generally have a 1 to 2 dog- per- table limit. Again, you should call ahead before showing up to make sure you will be accommodated.

Hotel managers, shopkeepers, festival producers and restaurant owners are becoming more willing to allow pet owners to bring their dogs along. At the same time, they are expecting you as the owner to act responsibly and to look after their best interests as well. Keep a close eye on your pet and anticipate any problems before they occur. This will be best for all involved.

Parenting Etiquette

Being a Good Role Model

Parents are the very first teachers in any child's life. When your child looks at you, no matter what you may think of yourself, he or she sees the person, values and behaviors he or she is to emulate. More specifically, when a daughter looks at her mother she makes determinations about womanhood. If her parents are together, she formulates opinions about what a wife is to be and how a wife relates to her husband. In like manner, the young male looks to his father for the information he needs about being a man. By studying his father's work ethics and behaviors, he is able to begin formulating his own perceptions about work, children and relationships.

As a parent you should endeavor to use the window in time that you have with your child in order to build and mold them into respectful and responsible adults who are well socialized and ready to make a difference in their world.

- **Help them to trust what you say.** As much as you are able you should make sure to follow through with any commitments or vows you make to your child. This includes being where you agree to be and allowing what you commit to allow. Even if the situation is a negative you should make sure you follow through. If you say that you are going to take your son's video console for one month if his grades do not improve next semester, make sure you take the video console if he doesn't deliver. This may cause tension and he may be angry for a while, but in the long run you'll win because he will respect you for doing what you said.
- **Be a person of integrity.** Make sure that your children know that you won't compromise your values and morals even if it cost you. If your boss asks you to do something unethical stand your ground and respectfully decline to participate. Use this as a teaching opportunity with your children and share with them that there may well be consequences for your decision. Help them to understand that there is never any reason to engage in corrupt activities.
- **Maintain good hygiene and practice healthy living.** If your children observe you living a healthy lifestyle that includes making wise food choices, exercising your body, regularly

brushing your teeth, and presenting yourself in a clean and respectful manner, he or she will model the same. They may not even realize they have taken on your habits but you'll be pleasantly surprised to see them living out what you have modeled.

- **Be a diligent worker.** You may have a career outside of the home or you may work inside the home. Whatever your vocation, be a hard worker who takes pride in what you do and who does their work well. Continue to be steadfast in your commitment to excellence in your work and your children will catch your work ethic. His or her work, as a child, is to complete his or her school work and any chores you have given. There should be an expectation that they do these well and consistently. Teach them to do their very best. This too will spill over into their adult life.

- **Respect other people.** There is no way of getting around the fact that as humans we interact with other humans. One of the key qualities necessary for maintaining good and healthy relationships with others is that of respect for others. Whether you are communicating with someone of your same social status, with a superior at work or with your domestic health, you should always be courteous and respectful. There is never any reason to be condescending and this is an important trait to pass on to your children. Much is made of bullying in our current society. This problem stems directly from a lack of respect. As you are respectful of others rights and feelings your children will learn to duplicate this character trait and present themselves to others as the classy person they are being trained to become.

Etiquette begins and ends with doing right by and to others. Keep these in mind as you live out your life before your children every day and I believe you will be pleasantly surprised by the honorable men and women you raise to adulthood.

How to Raise a Well-Mannered Child

"The children now love luxury; they have bad manners, contempt for authority; they show disrespect for elders and love chatter in place of exercise. Children are now tyrants, not the servants of their households. They no longer rise when elders enter the room. They contradict their parents, chatter before company, gobble up dainties at the table, cross their legs, and tyrannize their teachers. " -Author Unknown-

The above quote was inaccurately attributed to Socrates, a Greek philosopher who lived from 468-398 BC. If this quote is true it definitely supports the idea that there is nothing new under the sun—children have been misbehaving since the beginning of time. Having a child who is disrespectful can be a source of constant embarrassment and distress to a parent. Here are some helpful tips that a parent can use in order to instill good manners and honoring behavior in their children. Your child does not have to behave poorly; be encouraged and take action now. Remember that as adults we have the experience and grace to realize not to say the wrong thing. The key we must teach our children is to first be respectful in all things and to then think ahead before they open their mouths to speak.

Words of Encouragement and Advice:

Children need to be taught to live well and be honoring. If you are modeling rudeness and importunity at home do not expect your children to somehow turn out to be models of gracious behavior. Take responsibility for your child's behavior and do something about it. Respect is caught and your child will catch the fine art of being mannerly, well-spoken and respectful from your example and your discipline. If you teach your child at home that their inappropriate or rude remarks are cute and funny, he won't be able to discern the problem when he is out socially. Begin at home.

Give your youngster positive reinforcement. Children love praise; especially when it comes from a parent or loved one. Very often parents respond only to their children's undesirable behavior, ignoring their victories and positive actions completely. This choice may actually have the reverse result. Children want attention anyway they can get it—even if that means doing bad things. Encourage.

Five phrases that your child must master. *'Thank you.' 'Please?' 'May I …' 'Excuse me.' And 'No, thank you.'* No exceptions—these are required.

Be patient. Children are self-centered. Every parent recognizes this very early in the parenting charge. Again stay encouraged, just as with anyone learning how to do what is right, children need time to understand how to be mannerly. Teach them the importance of respecting others' feelings and needs and you will go a long way toward achieving this end. As they learn to listen more, speak less, esteem others and humble themselves their golden rule behavior will begin to shine forth.

Children are little people and should be respected and treated as such. These future leaders, moms, dads, teachers and who knows what else must be groomed for success and personal presentation. Don't neglect the opportunity to one day walk in the blessed knowledge and pleasure of one whose children are distinguished and honorable having a good name and reputation. Expect more; you won't be disappointed.

Learning how to respond graciously

"So teach us to number our days, that we may apply our hearts unto wisdom." The Holy Bible, - Psalm 90:12

I recently celebrated a birthday and as usual there were several people who felt they needed to ask my age. I know that there are many people who desire to be polite but do not want to reveal their age. I am one such person and contrary to popular belief everyone who declines to say is not vain. Vanity may be a motive for some, but many simply choose to keep their age as well as other vitals private. This choice may offend the one inquiring and that is regrettable; however, this is personal information and no one should fill pressured to answer. The elegant lady or gentleman must always consider another's comfort and should thus avoid questions that might cause them discomfort or embarrassment. Someone once said, *A lady never tells,* and I would like to add, *neither does she ask.*

As you attempt to live a life that is mannerly and socially graceful you should always place the needs of others first. In short, you should know that asking someone's age is rude, so you should not ask. If someone does ask you, know that it is completely proper for you to say something like, *"That is not information that I wish to share; I'm sure you understand."* Remain gracious and kind and move seamlessly to the next subject. Most people will not press the issue-although I have encountered some who are dogmatic about getting an answer. Just stand your ground and be assured in the knowledge that this is a rude question, one belonging in the same category as asking someone's weight, salary or even the carat weight of their diamond.

As a person who values manners and etiquette, realize that it is not your right to know personal details about others and neither should you feel obligated to share your own personal information. If you have been in the habit of asking others their age here are some things you might want to consider and implement.

- **Many people are very sensitive about their age;** as age related discrimination is a very real problem both in the social and work arenas. Many people respond differently even with prejudice or bias once they learn of one's biological age. Never let stereotypical ideas color your response to another.
- **Age is a state of mind.** I have had people think I was well over a decade younger than my actual age and experienced their shock when they learned my true numerical age. Never make assumptions about another person based solely on their age.
- There are those who are very mature behaving at twelve years and others who have lived five decades who do not have a clue about what is really important in life. **Never judge a person by his or her age.**
- As a gracious lady or gentleman your goal is to **consider others before yourself and seek their maximum comfort.** Never asking prying, inappropriate or intrusive questions is one way of achieving this goal.

Walking in confidence is one mark of a person of integrity who knows how to respond in any situation. She or he does so by exhibiting a dignity and self-assurance that others will not dare challenge. *Suffice it to say a lady (or gentleman for that matter) never asks and she (or he) doesn't need to tell.*

Etiquette Tips for Game Day

Three of my four daughters are competitive gymnasts. Now, to clarify I must add that although they are in the Junior Olympic categories they are all three compulsory level gymnasts. This means that they are learning the basics and not yet doing back flips on the balance beam! **These girls practice eight hours weekly all year round** in preparation for competitive meets. And like so many of you, guess who sits right there through the practices waiting, watching and bleacher style coaching? That's correct, I do. So, I really do understand the excitement parents feel on 'Game Day.' We're ready to see some results and for our little mini-me children to win some medals, games, or whatever it is they do in their sport.

Here's the Problem...

Too often we forget that the other parents sitting around us share our same enthusiasm about the game or event and that they are just as eager to see and enjoy their child's performance.

It comes down, once again, to personal style; Let yours shine even at the ball park.

On that wise, let's look at some ways we can lessen some of our fellow minor league sports fan's frustrations. Remembering to be thoughtful will go a long way toward making everyone's day at the ball park a little more pleasant.

5 Ways to Show Style during Your Child's Sports Event.

1. **Be Considerate and use the restroom before you take your seat.** This is important especially if you have little one's or a large family. It can be very inconvenient to have to keep getting up and down because the family beside you has eight children who can't seem to stay seated.
2. **Be Kind.** You never know who may be seated beside you so in order to avoid any problems keep your opinions and criticisms to yourself. Remember to do unto others as you would like for them to do unto you!
3. **Obey the Rules.** This can be difficult for some parents but I urge you to be good examples. In gymnastics, flash photography can be very dangerous. Even so, you would be surprised at how many parents flash away all during the meets.
4. **Allow the Coach to Coach.** It may seem like you have some tip to offer during the game that would be helpful--but take a deep breath and don't do it. It is rude to dishonor your child's coach in this public setting. If you really have a concern about his or her abilities you should schedule a private meeting with him or her at a more appropriate time to address your concerns.
5. **Be Mannerly.** Show your style and class by not being overly rowdy, boisterous or loud during the meet or game. You don't want to embarrass your child nor yourself so try to be reserved in your cheering and applause.

This list is by no means exhaustive, however ,if followed these simple yet gracious tips will go a long way toward building your reputation as a composed lady or gentleman who is considerate of others and who cares about their comfort.

Teaching Children Manners

It has been said by some that children are like sponges, they tend to soak up everything and every influence around them. Although Sociologists maintain that manners are unenforceable, it is very obvious that these standards or norms of behavior, if reinforced, can become a way of living for any child or adult. The key to teaching children to behave mannerly, as little ladies and gentlemen is instruction. Although we do not see as many 'Finishing Schools' thriving in our culture, teaching your child proper social grace, etiquette, intercultural competence, morality, politeness and more will go a long way toward aiding his or her success in life both socially and in business. Employers, friends, family and more like classy people. The mannerly person not only impresses others, but he or she is quick to commend another on their behavior. Manners are about respect and honor for self and for others.

Follow these helpful tips for teaching your own child manners.

1. **Model manners.** If you want your child to model manners, you must make sure you do as well. This is definitely not an area in which you can get them to do as you say and not as you do. First step to having a mannerly child is being a mannerly parent.
2. **Practice at home.** It is unrealistic for your child to just pick up the habit of good manners by telepathy. He or she needs to have lots of practice in the fine art of social graces. Take time to engage in role playing with your son or daughter. For instance, practice how to be courteous when using the telephone.
3. **Give him (or her) the words.** There are 5 words that should be among the first in every child's primary vocabulary. These should be used while speaking to children as young as 6 months old. Try this when your infant, toddler or young child tries to grab something from you, you withhold the item and direct them to ask politely. You say to them something like, "Say please." Or with an older child you might direct him or her to use the whole sentence and "Say, mom, may I please have a piece of cake?" Here are **five phrases that your child must master** 'Thank you.' 'Please?' 'May I ...' 'Excuse me.' And 'No, thank you.' No exceptions-these are required.
4. **Give your youngster positive reinforcement.** Children love praise; especially when it comes from a parent or loved one. Very

often parents respond only to their children's undesirable behavior, ignoring their victories and positive actions completely. This choice may actually have the reverse result. Children want attention anyway they can get it-even if that means doing bad things. Encourage.

5. **Be patient.** It is true that most children are self-centered by nature. Every parent recognizes this very early in the parenting charge. Again stay encouraged, just as with anyone learning how to do what is right, children need time to understand how to be mannerly. Teach them the importance of respecting others' feelings and needs and you will go a long way toward achieving this end. As they learn to listen more, speak less, esteem others and humble themselves their golden rule behavior will begin to shine forth.

6. **Learn to coach.** The field of Life Coaching is becoming more popular and needful. Many people are finding that they need someone to not only hold them accountable but to listen to their dreams, desires and assist them in goal setting. Help your child to establish social goals that will better equip him or her for daily interpersonal communication and interaction. It is no secret that people don't really like to be around others who are rude and obnoxious. No parent wants this for their child. Make a point to sit down and talk with them and listen to areas of struggle they may have when interacting with other people.

7. **Teach table manners.** There are many great manners and etiquette books available to assist you in getting table manners right. Once you understand the rules, be sure to share them with your son or daughter.

8. **Correct him or her on the spot.** Very young children often times don't realize what they are doing. For example, if you are speaking with a friend and your child interrupts you. Beg your friend's pardon and let your child know that his or her interruption is inappropriate. Or if your child calls an adult by his or her first name, take the moment to correct him or her. Make sure you use sensitivity in these types of situations. If you have an overly sensitive child you might want to excuse yourself and speak with him or her privately.

9. **Speak well.** Speech habits are so important. Often parents may sabotage their children's speech patterns by using slang and lazy habits themselves. Again, this is an area in which you need to model the correct behavior. Unless you want your child to speak in a sloppy, slang-ridden way, be well-spoken yourself.

10. **Lose the prejudices.** Your children are going to model your biases. If you hold strong opinions about a particular group or person, you should not make this a public point. No one has the right to interfere with the perfect liberties we hold as Americans, however, you don't want to perpetuate intercultural prejudices. Teach your children to judge a person by the 'content of their character' (Martin Luther King, Jr.) I hope these tips are helpful as you seek to teach your children to behave with manners and etiquette within society and in their daily lives.

Proper Behavior at the Symphony

Attending the symphony is always such an exciting experience. There is just something about the magnitude and dare I say majesty associated with the whole dynamic of being there. While preparing for the symphony there is a great since of excitement as you research the music, the composers and learn the history behind the particular performance you will be attending. Still the whole prospect of attending the symphony or any big concert production may seem a bit intimidating. Preparation and education are both key to minimizing any anxieties and optimizing your experience. Keeping this in mind here are some ways to prepare and remember too, if you are going to be taking children or novice symphony-goers along to the performance, you must take the time to acquaint them with symphony etiquette so that they might enjoy the experience as well.

Let's talk symphony. According to a wikipedia article, *"A symphony is an extended musical composition in Western classical music, arranged and scored almost exclusively for the orchestra. A symphony usually contains at least one movement composed according to the sonata principle. Many symphonies are tonal works in four movements with the first in sonata form, which is often described by music theorists as the structure of a "classical" symphony, although many symphonies by the acknowledged classical masters of the form, Joseph Haydn, Wolfgang Amadeus Mozart, and Ludwig van Beethoven do not conform to this model."*(Wikipedia)

The word symphony is derived from Greek συμφωνία, meaning "agreement or concord of sound", "concert of vocal or instrumental music", from σύμφωνος, "harmonious" (Oxford English Dictionary). The word was originally used to describe a reed instrument in the Bible or Torah book of Daniel. The Latin word symphonia was used to describe various instruments.

The normal four-movement form looks like this:

1. **First Movement** includes an opening sonata or allegro.
2. **Second Movement** includes a slow movement, such as adagio.
3. **Third Movement** includes a minuet with trio or the alternate Beethoven-style four-movement solo sonata": scherzo
4. **Fourth Movement** a final allegro, rondo, or sonata

The orchestra includes many kinds of instruments. Each has a different look and tone color. Think of each as a different home within your neighborhood housing a different family. Just as each home has a different name, the orchestra is made up of families too. The four families of the orchestra include: **The String Family** which are the violins, violas, basses and cellos. **The Percussion Family** includes the harp, piano, cymbals, triangles, timpanis, bass drum, snare drum and the marimba. **The Woodwind Family** is made up of the piccolo, flutes, oboes, English horn, bassoon, clarinets, bass clarinets, and the contrabassoon. **The Brass Family** has the French horns, trombones, tuba and trumpets.

Symphony Etiquette

*   **Arrival.** Patrons (that is you) should arrive no later than 30 minutes prior to the start of the performance. This will allow you and your party ample time to use the Hall's facilities, find seats, and settle in for the performance. In general, most halls open their doors 60 to 90 minutes before the concert.
*   **Silence Electronic Devices** Cellular phones, beepers, watches, electronic organizers, and any other noise-alarm device that might potentially disrupt the concert should be switched to silent mode or turned off.
*   **Attire.** I see a lot of misinformation about this one on the web. It is true that this may depend upon where you are attending the concert, however here are the general rules for dress at the symphony. Patrons of the symphony generally wear semi-formal, elegant, and business attire. On certain occasions such as an opening night **Formal** attire may be requested.
*   **Late Seating** is usually allowed during a convenient pause in the program. Please wait patiently for an usher to direct you accordingly.
*   **During the performance.** Once the concert has begun, guidelines to follow. **Don't talk, whisper, sing, hum, or move personal belongings.** Refraining from any and all of these will ensure that you, other patrons, and the performers enjoy the full benefits of the performance. **Don't enter or exit the hall while a performance is in progress.** Ushers are stationed at entrances

and exits and they will direct you. If you must leave your seat, do so quickly and quietly proceeding to the nearest door or if necessary asking the nearest usher for assistance.

- **Applause** If you are uncertain, follow the seasoned concert goers on this. Usually there is applause when the Concertmaster or orchestra first chair violinist enters the stage as well as when the conductor makes his entrance. During the actual performance you should only applaud at the close of a full piece of music. You should be able to determine these by looking over the program page which generally lists individual movements of longer compositions. In addition, the program notes should help you follow the orchestra's progress through each piece.
- **Children** Your particular hall or performance may have specific rules about children. Some concerts may be specifically designed for children or families with children under the age of 12 years. In either case you should make sure your child is capable of sitting quietly during a long performance. If you think this may be an issue you should probably not take them along.
- **During Intermission** you should take the time to visit the restroom, get a snack or other refreshment and visit briefly with other concert-goers. Watch for signs that you should return to your seat or adhere to the intermission time limits. Some halls will flash the lights or the doors may re-open.

An evening at the symphony hall offers concertgoers an opportunity to experience the power and passion of live music. This is an enriching occasion that everyone should enjoy at least once in a while. Prepare your heart and mind for a great adventure and enjoy the time spent taking pleasure in the sound of music.

Dining Etiquette

Forks, Spoons and Knives--Oh My!

It is so satisfying to be able to enter into a situation knowing that your social skills and etiquette are on point and ready to be demonstrated correctly. The socially graceful person is confident no matter where he or she finds him or herself. For many however, the occasional refresher course is a necessary commodity. Wherever you find yourself on the spectrum I hope this article will help you to be prepared to dine with confidence at your next formal dinner party. Identifying Each Piece

First things first; let us identify the utensils normally used during a formal dining experience. In most cases there are three (3) forks, two (2) knives and three (3) spoons. Always remember that the placement of your utensils offers a hint about their purpose and how to use them. During the formal meal you are expected to use your utensils from the outside in (moving toward the plate). This article will examine the American or Continental use of utensils while dining.

The Salad Fork is located closest to your napkin on the left side of your place setting. It is smaller than your Dinner Fork which is then located to the right of the salad fork and to the immediate left of your dinner plate. Just as the names suggest, the Salad Fork is to be used for your salad course and the **Dinner Fork** for your main dinner course. **The Cake Fork** is located at the top edge of your dinner plate and it should be used during the dessert course. You should hold your fork horizontally by balancing it between the first knuckle of the middle finger and the tip of the index finger while the thumb steadies the handle. Your left hand should then rest on your lap as you eat. If you are left-handed then you would rest your right hand as you eat.

There are three spoons used during a formal dinner party. The utensil located to the right of your plate on the outside is the **Soup Spoon**. This spoon is larger than the **Teaspoon** which is one place closer to the plate and slightly smaller. The third spoon at the setting is the **Dessert Spoon**. Like the cake fork, the dessert spoon is located at the top of the plate and below the place card and water glass. The spoon should also be held horizontally, balanced between the first knuckle of the middle finger and the tip of the index finger.

The knives at your place setting will be located one to the right of the plate and the other diagonally across the bread plate. **The Dinner Knife** is immediately next to the plate and should be used with the right hand if you are right-handed. It is used with the tip of the index finger leaning on the blade of the knife and you should be careful not to apply too much pressure; simply use it for control and to guide you as you cut your food. As you hold your food with the tines of your fork (now located in your left hand) in North America it is then customary to lay the knife across the top edge of your plate and switch your fork to the dominant hand, left or right. The **Bread Knife** should be used to butter your bread. You should never place soiled or used utensils back on the table cloth. These should always be placed on your dinnerware once they have been used; you wouldn't want to mess up your host's lovely table cloth.

Now here are some final tips for success and good measure!

- Place your napkin in your lap immediately upon being seated.
- You may rest your forearms on the table for support but never your elbows!
- Used utensils should be placed on the accompanying plate, but never on non flat surfaces such as bowls or teacups. For instance, when you have finished your soup, the spoon may be placed on either your salad or bread plate until the server clears the course.
- Never use a knife to cut your bread or salad. The Salad Fork has extra thick tines to enable you to cut tough or extra leafy salad ingredients. Your bread should always be torn apart.
- If you are having a conversation or taking a drink, place your utensil(s) on your plate during the pause.
- Enjoy your meal. Take a glance around and follow the example of your host or hostess. They are the norm and their mores should be esteemed.

Always remember great manners are great to have, use and see. Practice your skills so that you may relax and enjoy dinner knowing that you are put

What Should I Do If I Receive A Formal Dinner Invitation?

Question: What Should I Do If I Receive A Formal Dinner Invitation?

I just received an invitation to a dinner party and I don't know the hostess very well. Please list some helpful tips on what to do next.

Answer:

Dinner parties are great fun. They offer a chance to get out and interact with your friends and loved ones, meet new people and of course try delicious new food. When you are invited remember that there are some specific guest 'no-no's' to keep in mind.

Once you have received an invitation to dinner **and** you have checked your calendar to make sure you are available you should **respond to the host.** This may be done either by mail, telephone or email if you like. During your conversation remember that this is not your dinner party and you should not specify any food likes, preferences or dislikes. Ask if there is any way you might be helpful and if you are uncertain of the attire for the evening, ask. A dinner party is a great time to wear some of your more dressy outfits. Once you know the type of dinner, you may have a better idea of what to wear. Once you have decided, pull out all the stops and do your best to look good. Be stylish and elegant but, remember to consider your comfort. There seems to be a direct correlation between hurting feet and a bad attitude. Remember, you want to be a great guest who is pleasant to be around.

Arrive to the dinner on time. Once you are there prepare to abide by the host's agenda. **Sit according to the place card directions** and don't be fussy about the arrangements. If you happen to be served something that you cannot or do not eat, simply eat around it without comment.

Wait for the host or person of honor to begin eating before you do. If someone asks you to pass a particular dish, set it beside the next person's plate asking them to pass it to the person. This continues person to person until it arrives at the original requester.

When all is said and done, don't forget to **have a great time.** After the party a nice thank you note is appropriate thus letting the hosts know just how much you enjoyed the evening.

How to Use Your Napkin When Dining

When one is dining the napkin is an important part of the experience. Not only is it handy for blotting spills and patting your mouth, but it is also handy when you need to clean your hands. Here are some etiquette tips for using your napkins when you are eating.

Using your napkin at a restaurant

Once you have arrived at the restaurant and you have been seated the next thing you should do is **remove your napkin from its place, unfold it and place it on your lap.** This is where you should keep it until you need it. Take the time to unfold rather than shake the napkin open before placing it on your lap. In some restaurants the wait person may provide this service for you. This is a matter of preference and it is okay if you do this on your own instead of allowing the waiter to place it for you.

- **The napkin should remain on the lap until either it is needed or the meal ends.** You should never use the napkin to clean your silverware, nor should you wipe your face with it. In addition, should you need to blow your nose, excuse yourself from the table and dining area and use your handkerchief. This is not an appropriate use of the dinner napkin.
- If you need to excuse yourself from the table, you should use one hand to grab the napkin and then loosely fold the napkin, placing it to the left or right of your plate. There is no need to refold your napkin, but **try not to crumple it or make it into a ball.** Never leave the napkin on the chair or on the floor.
- At the end of the meal, leave the napkin semi-folded at the left side of the place setting or on the plate. Either of these moves will signal to the wait staff that you have completed that course.

Using your napkin at a private dinner party:

The formal or dinner party meal officially begins once the host or hostess unfolds his or her napkin. This is a signal to all of the guests to follow in suit. Once again, unfold your napkin and place it on your lap. You may leave it folded lengthwise if it is a large dinner napkin.

- As with restaurant dining, the napkin should remain on the lap until you either need to be excused for some purpose or the meal ends.
- You should watch the host or hostess closely during the meal. He or she will generally signal the end of the meal by placing his or her napkin on the table. Once the meal is over, you too should end your meal and signal you have done so by placing your napkin neatly on the table to the left of your dinner plate. Remember there is no need to attempt to refold the napkin as it is considered soiled and will need to be laundered.

Whether you are dining in a fancy restaurant or in the humble home of a dear friend, you should try to be courteous and neat as you eat. Your napkin is there for your use during the meal if you should need it. These tips offer some guidelines on what is generally expected with napkin use.

Quick Answers to Dining Etiquette Questions

Being invited to a formal or casual dinner party can be both exciting and nerve wrecking at once. It's great to be going, but too often we are left to wonder what to do and what not to do once we have arrived. Most hosts and hostesses invite their friends and family to their homes in order to have a great time and enjoy good food and friendly fellowship together. Try not to get upset about the event and realize that you company is desired and your host or hostess is looking forward to spending a great evening together with you and a group of his or her close friends. Just in case you need a few refresher tips on what is expected during the evening, here are some general social and dining etiquette rules for dinner parties.

- **Follow whatever dress code is suggested** by your host or hostess on your invitation.
- **Be punctual,** ideally you should try to arrive at least 10 minutes before the announced start time. Make every effort not to arrive late.
- **Come bearing gifts.** It is polite to bring a token hostess gift. Try to avoid flowers, candy or any other food item that the host or hostess will feel obliged to share during the party. You should not expect your gift to be used or served during the dinner party.
- **Follow the host or hostesses lead during the evening.** During a formal dinner party there will normally be name cards and the seating will typically be a man then a woman alternately around the table. The women are generally seated to the right of the men

and it is not uncommon for couples to be seated apart. If there are no cards, wait for the host or hostess to indicate where you are to sit.

- Some homes and families offer a prayer or blessing as their custom prior to each meal. As a dinner guest you should **feel free to either join in the prayer or sit respectfully silent** during their expression. If a toast is offered, you should join in. If the host or hostess stands then so should you.
- **The serving of the tea or coffee will signify that the formal dinner has concluded.** At this point you should feel free to either leave or mingle. Again, watch the host and hostess for clues about their expectations.
- Always remember to **send a handwritten thank you note** to the host or hostess after a formal dinner party.

Part of the great enjoyment of going to a dinner party is enjoying the great conversation and laughter with friends and acquaintances. Be yourself and do your part to make the evening one that all will remember for a long time.

Tipping: Who, When and How Much

It is not always easy to remember who we should tip. In addition, sometimes we don't know exactly when to tip. Here are some quick tips on tipping that should help you navigate everyday situations at home and abroad!

In general you should tip the following individuals for services rendered to you and if at all possible these should be given directly to the individual, in cash, and with a gracious 'Thank You.'

- Restaurant **Server.** I'm sure this one is no surprise. The normal amount should range between 15 to 20 percent and should be given at the conclusion of the meal. If at all possible you should try to give the tip directly to the server along with a thank you and in cash.
- Hotel **Maid & Concierge.** I am afraid that many people are not aware that maids are to receive a **daily** tip from hotel guests. This should be at least $2 dollars per day. The Concierge may be

tipped if he/she assists you and don't forget to tip you Bellman. He should receive $1-2 dollars per piece of luggage.

- When you receive any **salon services** you should tip. These services include nails, hair and massage. Depending upon the service you receive tip between 18 to 20 percent of the fee.
- Your **Valet** should receive at least $2 dollars. This should be given after your keys are returned to you.
- Please tip the **Pizza Delivery Person**. Much like wait staff the delivery worker depends heavily upon tips to make a decent living. He or she should also receive at least $2 dollars.
- When you are moving, don't forget to tip your **Movers** this should be around $50 for the foreman and around $20 for each additional worker

Just a note-- don't worry if you are on a cruise your daily tips are normally included in your costs. This is a lot to remember. My advice is that you invest in a wallet sized tipping chart for convenience and remember be gracious and generous to those who've served you!

Entertainment Etiquette

The Art of Being a Great Host or Hostess

Ralph Waldo Emerson said the following about etiquette, "Manners are the happy way of doing things," and I have to agree. Having and practicing good manners does indeed make people happy and even goes a long way toward improving their quality of life. When one is mannerly and accomplished in the etiquette of entertaining, he or she is confident and able to enjoy just being. I believe this is because we are blessed ourselves when we are given the opportunity to serve and give to others. That is why I recommend spreading the joy by learning to host dinners and parties often. Entertaining at home is a great way to enjoy good friends and fun fellowship for any good reason you can perceive.

Once you have mastered the art of setting a grand table and the fundamentals of table manners, it's time to start planning and hosting your own celebrations and dinner parties. The key to delightful entertaining is to remember your goal, which should be to provide a pleasurable and accommodating experience that your guests will remember and cherish. If you attain this goal, you won't ever have difficulty having enough guests at your parties. Here are some tips to get you started.

- **Start small** in order to gain some practical experience. Why not host an intimate casual party and build on that particular platform in the future. This type of party will go a long way toward helping you understand party and hostess dynamics.
- **Co-host** alongside a relative or friend if you don't feel you are quite ready to go it alone. This is a great idea for parties such as a large gathering, formal dinner, social event or an athletic banquet. If this seems like a great first step for you, simply volunteer and pitch in where you can. You will be amazed at how much you'll pick up.
- **Pick a theme** and then roll with it. There are so many unique and fun possibilities when you are hosting an event. For instance, you can host a post-election party or you could host an outdoor sports party or tournament. Another great idea is a worthy cause party or dinner. You could even host an ethnic heritage dinner during which you explore foreign cuisine.

- **Plan and prepare,** for your sake and your guests. Your friends and family will not enjoy your party if you are stressed from exhaustion and weariness. Your attitude and demeanor should set the tone for the party. If you are too tired, your guests might even feel guilty for causing you so much work and they might even bow out early.
- **Decide on your menu.** Once you have set your theme your menu should be narrowed enough to not be too overwhelming. Grab your favorite cookbook and your recipe files and write up some mock menus. Once you have narrowed down the choices, you will probably want to practice making the dishes over the course of the next couple of weeks so that you are versed at what to expect, and how much your recipe really yields and more.
- **Set your budget** remembering that there are quite a few associated costs in party-planning. Now that you have your menu, you can price your grocery list. Next, you'll need to decide on your decoration costs. If you are going to have fresh flowers, get online and price your choices. You may want to buy wholesale and arrange them yourself. If you will need paper products such as plates, napkins and cups add those as well. When it is time to shop you should try to buy in bulk in order to get the best per person deals.
- **Engage help** from other people. Ask your best friend, sister, brother or another person you know who would be willing to help you with cooking or preparations on the day of the party. If you don't have additional help, again you must prepare in such a way that you don't complete exhaust all of your energy the day of the event.

I hope you are able to find ways this year to celebrate others and host great parties. People really do love having an excuse to dress up and use their manners just because they can. I encourage you to find a reason to entertain. Now you should have the etiquette to do so graciously.

Holiday Entertaining

Valentine's Day a time to share the love

February fourteenth is celebrated as Valentine's Day in the United States. During this holiday couples and friends, parents and children shower others with love notes, candy, flowers and more as a show of their love and appreciation for them. There are many opportunities to participate in the Valentine's Day festivities; however every gift is not appropriate for every person or in every situation.

Here are some helpful suggestions for buying and receiving Valentine's Day gifts.

- For married couples the sky is the limit on what you can and/or should give. Some of the more traditional gifts include: **a bouquet of one dozen roses, diamonds,** and **candy.** A fur coat or another extravagance is always well-received and usually very unexpected. For a unique twist why not try **tickets to the theater,** or a trip to the big city. You might want to hire a housekeeper for the week or sponsor a day at an expensive day spa.
- For those who are dating why not try a gift that is not embarrassingly intimate or personal, but one that you know your friend might like very much. These types of gifts might include items such as flowers, a new clothing item he or she has been wanting, candy, a card, chocolates or another gift that isn't overly expensive and won't cause uneasiness or feelings of obligation that might be premature. Remember that your date may feel badly if his/her gift doesn't measure up to yours so you should keep this in mind.
- For children who are buying for teachers you might want to purchase a nice pin or some stationery. You can also send a flower or a box of chocolates. For the class exchange why not let them exchange candy and little homemade or store bought notes. Keep them appropriate and find out how the teacher has specified they are to be distributed. He or she may want you to leave them unaddressed so that they can place them all in a collective basket or something like that.
- For parents who want to buy for their children or parents the options are limitless. Children love surprises. You might want to take them out to dinner and/or a movie in lieu of a romantic dinner for two. Children might also enjoy learning the history of the day and celebrating together with family and friends during a family dinner party in honor of love. For older parents why not send them on an all-expense paid trip or a romantic weekend in the country at a bed and breakfast. They might also enjoy a thoughtful card accompanied by a fruit basket or tickets to symphony. If your parents are sports fans you might buy them some tickets to see their favorite team play.

The important thing to do is to remember the purpose of the day is to show love and appreciation for our loved ones. What a great opportunity to find unique and creative ways to bless them with your kindness, generosity and love.

Hosting a Great Super Bowl Party

Capping off the football season is yet another honor given to January each year. The Super Bowl game is the most watched sports event in the world. It is also a great time for friends and football fans to come together and enjoy a festive party as they watch the big game. Your Super Bowl party can be an all-day event or one that begins right before the kick-off and ends at the game's conclusion. Whichever you decide, you should definitely have a plan and enlist the help of your friends in order to have the best party yet.

Here are some tips for game day success.

- **Set up two televisions** in at least two rooms. You may even want to place another screen in the kitchen or where the buffet is set up (if it is away from the main party rooms). Use one room for serious viewers who are not likely to want to do or hear a lot of talking during the game. The other room might be best for bowl-game only fans that will be there for the socializing, food and fun. They will still want to see the game and the half-time show, but they will definitely want to enjoy and discuss the infamous Super Bowl commercials. If children have been included it would be nice to set up an area just for them as well. If they are too young to really appreciate the game, place them somewhere safe and near that offers them the freedom to play and enjoy the party in their own way.
- **Serve party favorites** and remember this is definitely not the time for fancy dishes. Try to think convenience and finger foods. You'll want to prepare items that aren't too messy and are able to be consumed quickly. Invite guests to bring something along such as some chicken wings, pizza, chips, or soda pop. If you are planning to serve any alcoholic beverages you should prepare to collect your guests keys at the beginning of the party. It might be safer to serve sodas, tea and non-alcoholic drinks so that you don't have to worry about anyone over-indulging and leaving your home and party intoxicated. It is also a great idea to have lots of napkins and paper towels on hand for any messy

situations. Remember your guests will be having a good time and they might be a bit animated during the game. All of their activity might equal spills.

- **Decorate according to the game.** This might include the game number or the team colors. Make sure you have appropriate signage in your yard and always advise your neighbors that you are having a party and that your guests will be parking on the street. It is totally your call as to whether or not you invite your neighbors, it would be a nice gesture, but invite them only if you feel comfortable around them.
- **Respect the host's rights** to the remote control and the main chair. He or she has been preparing all day (and then some) for this party. Be a courteous guest and leave his or her remote control alone. In addition, let your hosts have the best seats in the house. If you are the host, try to make sure that your seating has the best visibility options possible. Theater style would be great but if you don't have this type, be creative.
- **Pregame activities** are always needful. If you are hosting an all day party think of some ways to entertain your guest before the game begins. If you have a pool and live in a warm climate, have a pool party. Other options might include team trivia games or engaging in great conversations about the season. Refrain from making assumptions about your guests. Don't assume that all men are knowledgeable about football or that all women aren't. Mind your etiquette and make every effort not to be offensive toward the other team's fans. Try not to be too over-bearing about your team, this is not the time to brag and boast too much, this is a time to have fun and enjoy good company, great food and the game of the season.

New Year's Eve Celebrations That Include Children

New Year's Eve parties and celebrations are known to be a bit over-the-top when compared to the other more family-oriented holidays like Christmas and Thanksgiving. For many adults this is a time to put on their finest (and most expensive) clothes and party the night away. There are usually many events to choose from as this is a popular time to host balls and fundraising events. Still, there are some families who would prefer to spend their first hours of the New Year with their family members-- including their children. This is especially true for newly married couples with small children or retirees who no longer have an office party to attend. If you won't be able to get to Times Square in New York City this year I've got a few suggestions for your end of the year celebration.

Why not take this opportunity to try something new in celebration of the New Year. How about:

- **Going to church.** If you are a member of a church or another faith community, many of them hosts special services during New Year's Eve. There may still be loud music, in celebration, but you won't deal with unruly people under the influence whose behavior may offend young children.
- **Going on a vacation.** Wouldn't your family love to take a trip to Disney for New Year's Eve? Or you might want to plan a cruise for the occasion. If you choose to do something extravagant like traveling, you'll want to be sure to plan ahead; depending upon the size of your family this could be an expensive choice.
- **Watching movies.** If your children are at the 'best friends' stage, you might want to volunteer to host a New Year's Eve slumber party for him or her and a few close friends. They can watch movies (under close supervision) and play video games while having their favorite snacks and more.
- **Going camping.** If you live in a warmer climate, this could be a perfect time to take a camping trip away from the bright lights and enjoy the calmness of nature. If you have close friends who also have children, why not rent an RV and take a long weekend trip to a favorite national park for the holiday together.
- **Having a dinner party.** Do you really ever need to have a reason to invite friends and family over for a fun get together? This can be a great time of playing board games, eating, swimming, or whatever else your group enjoys doing when they are together.

No matter how you choose to spend your New Year's Eve, be sure that you face the New Year with a great attitude and with hope for the best. This is not a time to sulk and but an opportunity for renewed hope and faith. Decide that you will put the past behind you and embrace the future, with your family at your side, in the spirit of celebration, fun and expectancy.

Thanksgiving Day Entertaining: Preparing More than the Turkey

The consummate host or hostess should always be well prepared in every way to deal with the complexities that tend to accompany big dinner parties. Surprisingly many people may not view the annual Thanksgiving Day dinner as a dinner party. The truth is that if you are the person hosting your family or friends this year, you are hosting a big dinner party. We can all agree, that the holidays can be a bit overwhelming. Your goal as an experienced host or hostess should be to create an atmosphere that is welcoming, food that is delicious and pleasant to the eye and an agenda that guides but is not restrictive. Bear in mind that your guests don't want to get dressed up, travel a long or short distance to your home, wait for others to arrive and then eat during a boring uninspired dinner. There is so much more to serving up a great Thanksgiving Day buffet than preparing the meals.

One of the things I would recommend the elegant host or hostess do prior to the dinner is to brush up on his or her Thanksgiving Day history. For instance, did you know that historians say that the tradition of celebrating before and after the cycles of the harvest was a well established European tradition before their arrival in North America? The Europeans would hold great festivals in celebration in order to give thanks for the harvest and to rejoice with their neighbors after a season of hard work. Another frequent question that tends to come up during the day is about the origins of the holiday. You should know that "Thanksgiving or Thanksgiving Day, which is traditionally celebrated in the United States on the fourth Thursday in November, was first deemed a holiday by federal legislation in 1941, and it has been an annual tradition in the United States by presidential proclamation since 1863 and by state legislation since the Founding Fathers of the United States."(Wikipedia) As a good host or hostess you should have plenty of conversation starters that will encourage your guests to interact and enjoy lively fellowship.

Here are some additional ways to insure your dinner party is a success.

- **Keep your dinner guest list manageable.** If this is your first time hosting a big meal, perhaps you should confine your list to your immediate family members rather than branching out to include friends and acquaintances. Your family members will be more patient with any lapses in your hostess duties and because they are family, you will be less stressed if anything does go wrong. Of course the exception might be your mother or mother-in-law. If you receive criticism from either, remember they are most likely only trying to be helpful and receive the advice graciously.

- **Consider enlisting a caterer.** The last thing you want to happen during your Thanksgiving Day festivities is for you to wind up stressed and wearied due to fatigue. One way to avoid this might be to consider purchasing some items from a professional. Why not prepare the turkey, ham and or roast as well as some of the popular sides such as: potato salad, greens, green beans, mashed potatoes, rolls, dressing/stuffing, macaroni and cheese, cranberry relish and pickled eggs. You could then purchase several specialty desserts and fruit platters from a professional caterer or grocer. People are more likely to complain about a bad dessert than any other part of the meal.

- **Enlist a helper.** This could be your teenage daughter or son or another friend with whom you can trade tasks. You make a super sized serving of macaroni and cheese and she makes a double batch of rolls. It is important that you recognize your limits so don't try to be superwoman or man.

- **Hire a professional cleaning service.** Depending upon the size of your get together, your home might just be overly occupied during the morning, afternoon and evening. After a day of serving and entertaining, you will probably be nearly exhausted. Unless they offer, you probably won't want to ask any of your guests to help you clean and straighten. If you plan ahead, you could arrange for a team of maids to come in on the Friday or Saturday after the event and do a super cleaning for you. You could even confine their efforts to certain areas like the kitchen, dining area, family room, powder room and recreation area.

- **Relax and enjoy** However you decide to conduct your dinner party, you should resolve to relax and enjoy the company of your guests. It is very rude to invite others to your home and then mistreat or act impatiently with them. Your guests will take their clues from your attitude and behavior, so be sure to put on your best smile as well as your kindest heart.

I hope these tips are helpful and that your Thanksgiving Day dinner is a huge success.

Help! I Need Conversation Starters for My Party.

Question: Help! I Need Conversation Starters for My Party

I just hate it when my dinner parties have one of those awkward extended silences during the meal. Do you have any ideas on how to prevent these from happening?

Answer:

One of the most difficult responsibilities associated with hosting a successful dinner or social gathering might just be keeping the conversation flowing. Here are some great trivia bits that will aid in your efforts to entertain your guests. Use these when you need to get the communication rolling again or as conversation starters during the meal.

These questions and more are formulated from information found within and courtesy of the game Sybarit

1. **Are you serving chicken for dinner?** Why not offer this trivia bit of information. In culinary circles, the left chicken thigh is said to be the most tender.
2. **With an after dinner treat such as ice cream** you can share with your guests that ice cream (more specifically sorbet) was first made in China.
3. **For guests from the younger *specialty coffee* generation** you might want to share that a percolator was once the the appliance used to make coffee. Or how about this bit of information. Many people worry over the amount of caffeine found in a can of Coca-Cola. Did you know that one can has the same amount of caffeine as a half a cup of coffee?
4. **Mixing dinner and a movie?** Woody Allen fans might enjoy this seafood quote. This famous funny man was once quoted as saying "I will not eat oysters. I want my food dead, not sick, not wounded, but dead!"
5. **There are so many great food options** available to the American host/hostess. Share this bit of trivia as a side dish to your Sushi. Do your guests know the origin of this raw fish/seaweed delicacy? Why its Japan of course.
6. **That great new menu you're considering lists a roux.** Any thoughts on what that is? Roux is a mixture of butter or other

fatty substance and flour that is often used in Cajun inspired dishes.

7. **Who doesn't love a great salad.** Here's a great trivia bit about greens. Did you know that the common weed, Dandelion, may be eaten in salads and used to make wine? Its a fact.
8. **Impress your guests with your extensive vocabulary** all while enjoying some hot chili peppers. The unit used to describe the heat level of a chili pepper is termed Tempranillo.
9. **Are your guests inquiring about your marzipan?** Make sure they and you know that the minimum amount of almond paste in real marzipan is fifty-percent. This information will sure come in handy in the event your guests share any food allergies.

Hosting friends and family is such an enjoyable event. I hope your dinner goes well and remember, these trivia items are not meant to be used to boast but to help you steer your party conversations should there be a lack of interesting things to talk about. Research these and more trivia nibbles and use them as prompts, allowing the conversation to flow from the results

Cooking Etiquette

Sanitary Cooking Tips for Hosts

It an awful thought, but every year approximately 87 million people suffer from cases of food poisoning. Of those who are affected, there are an average of 371,000 hospitalizations and an appalling 5,700 deaths. Keeping these statistics in mind, it is wise to take care that you are necessarily clean and sanitary as you prepare food for others. Cooking etiquette is serious business as you would not want anyone to feed or offer you food that has been mishandled or cooked in less than sanitary conditions.

Here are some courteous food safety tips to be considered and used as you prepare meals and parties for your guests.

Think cleanliness. There are some things about cooking that should become second nature to you. Cleanliness is a non-negotiable in food prep. Do what you need to do to insure your counters and cooking areas are clean. If you are using a wooden cutting board, it should be cleaned with hot soapy water and vinegar in order to make sure any bacteria has been removed. Clean your faucets and counters often with anti-bacterial spray and/or bleach. Cover your hair with a net or cap in order to avoid getting hair into the food. If you must use the restroom while cooking, be extra vigilant about cleaning your hands and fingernails before returning to cook. Here's a little trick--wash your hands (including the areas under your nails and between your fingers) with hot soapy water while singing through the children's song, "Twinkle, Twinkle Little Star." A verse of this song usually lasts about 30-40 seconds which is about how long you need to make sure you are cleaning your hands well.

Think temperature. Paying attention to temperatures is very important when dealing with food safety. In general, your refrigerator should be set at 40 degrees Fahrenheit or colder and your freezer should be kept at or below zero degrees. A good meat thermometer is probably one of your best kitchen investments. Remember that chicken (or any other poultry) is safe to eat after the white meat reaches a temperature of at least 170 degrees, and when dark meat reaches at least 180 degrees. When poked, poultry juices should run clear without any tinge of red or pink. When preparing beef, pork, lamb or ground meats you should cook until the meat reaches a minimum of 165 degrees Fahrenheit.

Think dates. If something in your recipe is past it's recommended 'use by' date, don't chance using it. Even if the item looks or smells okay, these are not sufficient monitors of the food item's real condition. It will be difficult for you to tell whether an item has gone bad by using your senses so it is best that you trust the label. If it is expired, toss it.

Think cold and hot. When you are serving, take care to keep cold foods as chilled and hot foods hot; lukewarm is not the goal. Try not to leave any food, whether hot or cold out any longer than two hours. If you have any leftovers, they should be consumed or tossed within three days.

In the unlikely event that someone does become ill after eating at your home, etiquette dictates that you take a proactive stance and make sure to accept full responsibility. If this was a large party, you will need to check with your other guests in order to advise them that one of the guests became ill after the meal. Be apologetic and offer to assist the person in any way you can.

Shopping Etiquette

How to Shop with Style at Christmas

It is true that Christmas time is probably the most wonderful time of the year. We love this season for so many reasons. Beginning with the thankfulness and giving that comes along with the Thanksgiving Holiday, extending throughout the month of December and into the beginning of the New Year, there seems to be a special excitement that over takes us as we love, enjoy, dine, serve, give and receive.

One favorite stylish and unique to the season part of the many traditions involves shopping for and giving to other people. Etiquette is all about doing things well and interacting with others in such a way that they are better and happier because you did. As you prepare to shop til you drop, here are some great shopping etiquette tips on where and how to shop smart.

- **Plan Ahead** and you will go a long way toward saving big. Beginning as early as October, many stores, in an attempt to get the jump on the Black Friday sales, will begin offering fantastic one-day or weekend sales. In addition, if you are the kind that can keep a secret, it is wise to shop throughout the year. Many savvy shoppers even shop for the next year's presents on the day after Christmas. Stores are anxious to clear their shelves of overstock so this is a great option if you have gift ideas in mind that early.
- **Pay It Smart.** Even if you are not having any financial difficulties and you are secure in your employment, it is wise not to go into debt buying gifts. Set a budget and stick to it. This is another reason to start your shopping early. Choose items that you can either afford to pay for in cash or lay-a-way. Many stores such as ToysRUs ® and Walmart ®, which carry children's items such as toys and electronics, offer lay-a-way plans that don't require you to pay the final balance until right before the Christmas holiday.
- **Be Unique** Gift giving and receiving can be stressful, but it doesn't have to be that way. Use your creativity to find unique ways to surprise the recipients on your list. For instance, think outside the box. Let's say you only have $20 to spend on your cousin, Homer. You happen to know that he loves to ski. Let's say you know how to knit and you know that a cashmere sweater is out of your price range. Buy some very nice cashmere yarn and

knit him a nice sweater. You will have to plan ahead, but who wouldn't love a well made, cashmere sweater for their next ski trip?

- **Relative Expense.** When you are shopping for an adult you know very well, this is a great opportunity to be creative and splurge. Here's what I mean. If you know that your aunt loves to journal then think about what you can buy that is really expensive for what it is, but still within your budget. Those who journals are always in need of a new journal or a nice pen. If your budget for the gift is $25, then find an expensive journal or pen for that amount. Your normal journal might cost $5-8, but if you buy one for $25 it will probably be a very nice and expensive one that she probably wouldn't purchase for herself.

- **Extraordinary Buys** As you make out your shopping list, consider buying gifts that are unique and out of the ordinary. Something that you know your recipient will really appreciate and something that he or she probably would never buy for themselves even if they liked it. Here is an example, last year for Christmas my aunt gave me a card. When I opened I read that she had purchased some animals in my family's name as a donation to a family in a Third World country. I was very blessed to receive such a gift. I had looked at those particular advertisements many times but had never purchased one. Think of something extraordinary and really surprise someone this year.

- **Stick to the List** Children are very specific about what they want. If the children on your list have named a particular item, you will do well to stick to the list. As a parent, I have had to learn this lesson the hard way. It is very easy to go to the toy store and see a million things that little Colton is going to love, only to find out that he will only play with the one $5 dollar battery operated radio that he saw and fell in love with. If you are buying for nieces and nephews and grandchildren, heed this advice. They usually really do know what they want.

I hope that you have as much fun shopping for loved ones this year as I am planning to have. This truly is a wonderful time of the year.

Communication Etiquette

How to Deal With Conflict in a Relationship

You are able to read this article right now because you have learned to communicate through the understanding of written language. All communication can be classified into three categories; these include speaking, listening and understanding. Communication Etiquette therefore involves courteous and well-thought out interaction between individuals or groups that includes informed speech, attentive and active listening and a sincere grasp or understanding of what is being communicated.

One common cause for the breakdown of communication between friends, within families or amongst co-workers is the introduction of conflict or a difficulty. In these instances, the person of etiquette, should desire to resolve the conflict and move on as quickly as possible in order to resume a right relationship with any and all of those involved. Others will recognize you as a fair-minded, logical communicator with leadership qualities when you take the lead in resolving conflicts within relationships.

Here are some **Principles for Solving Problems** you can use in your everyday life in order to get along, influence and communicate better within your sphere of influence.

- **Know and Embrace why you believe the conflict needs to be resolved.** It is important that you have a conviction or belief about why this particular conflict is unhealthy and unnecessary and needs to be dealt with immediately. It is true that some amount of conflict may be needful in some situations in order to facilitate or cause change. For instance, if your teen-aged daughter continuously oversleeps and causes the house to be in a frenzied state before work and school, perhaps choosing to allow some healthy conflict will cause her to change her behavior. How about letting her deal with some consequences such as a family that is disappointed in her lack of respect for everyone else and has determined to let her know that they find her constant tardiness to be rude behavior. On the other hand, most conflict is destructive and disruptive and should be dealt with immediately. Is the conflict causing discord in the workplace? Is the problem affecting productivity? Make up your mind why this is a problem to be handled immediately and proceed from there.

- **See the good in the conflict** Decide what good, if any, can or has come from the conflict and use that to increase your knowledge of human relationships and intra-personal communication. As a result of conflict, there is often a great deal of emotional growth.
- **Determine your goal** and **Start with yourself** You don't want to attempt to resolve a conflict having ulterior motives. Be clear within your own mind about why you feel it is important to restore the relationship and examine your heart and motives. Ask yourself what role you played in the conflict and deal honestly with your own feelings, failures and faults.
- **Humble yourself and seek and give forgiveness.** Pride will prove to be a stumbling block to reconciliation every time. Be sure to be transparent in your communication, speak truth, listen to the needs and perceptions of the others and relate that you understand by restating their concerns and needs.
- **Deal with the problem, don't ignore it.** It may be difficult to deal with a problem head on, but this is the only way to move past it and move on. If the attempt at reconciliation is marked by shallow apologies and vague references there will be no real resolve. State the actual problem and then deal with ways to overcome the difficulty. If your co-worker constantly does the bare minimum at work, causing you to carry more than your fair share of the work-load, it is important to let him or her know that this is causing a problem with how you respect or perceive him or her and that you are becoming resentful of his or her lackadaisical attitude toward the bottom-line at work. Handling this issue sooner rather than later will enable you to communicate in a polite manner. If you wait, things might get ugly.
- **Try not to nit-pick.** Determine whether this is a real problem rather than a mere annoyance. If you consider the situation carefully and recognize that this conflict is really just a difference of opinion, you may want to just let it pass. Change your mind about the situation and recognize that people have little quirks and differences, but this is definitely not a cause for major conflict and disharmony.

Solving problems is definitely something that the person of etiquette wants to be known for doing well. As leaders in the social setting, you want it to be known that you are a level-headed thinking versus emotional responder to whatever life may present. As you go through life you will find that people will respect you and your opinions and see you as a person they can trust to be fair and honest.

Let's Go To the Movies

Americans love our entertainment. Whether we are watching a new film or listening to the orchestra at our favorite symphony house, we long to be amused in our spare time. It is great for the economy and for individuals and families to get out on the town and enjoy the arts and entertainment available in their community. When you are out you want to remember that etiquette is very important within a society. It is very true that etiquette and use of manners is really only missed when it is not present. Do you think about how kind the person who speaks to you is or do you really only give the matter any thought when you meet up with someone who either does not respond or who responds inappropriately? Have you noticed that we usually only take note of behavior that is unexpected and lacks etiquette?

When you go to the movies, here are some Urban Etiquette Tips to keep in mind.

- **When you attend a movie** at the local cinema house you should always remember that the audience came to see, hear and enjoy the actors in the film and not you. I am aware that many people think it is very funny when they talk to the actors on the screen and keep a running dialogue during a movie, however this is not true. Even if you receive a few laughs the novelty will wear off very quickly and you will find that your behavior is bothersome to most of the other movie-goers.
- **Please do not save seats** at the opening of a blockbuster new film. If you and all of the other patrons had to wait in line or order your tickets early so should your friends and/or family members. Of course, if your spouse, date or friend went to the restroom or to the concession stand you should definitely reserve his or her seat.
- **Realize your role** as an audience member you are there to enjoy the film. You should avoid criticizing the movie, director, actors, soundtrack or any other part of the production you find objectionable out loud while you are there. If you feel you have a real issue you should either leave the theater or take the time to contact the studio, write and editorial or blog about the film and why you were displeased or offended.

106

- **Hold the applause.** Applause is an acknowledgement from the audience members to the actors or performers, that they have been pleased with the production. During any form of live entertainment this is appropriate and expected. However, when you are attending a movie there is really no need or place for applause. The exceptions to this rule might include special performance screenings during which the actors and producers, filmmaker or director are present.
- Use discretion with rude audience members. If you happen to encounter an audience member who is being obnoxious or engaging in rude behavior, it is perfectly acceptable for you to try to remedy the situation by giving a quick, but stern glance his or her way. If that method fails to persuade them, ask them politely if they could stop the behavior. Any additional complaints should be taken directly to the management or the usher for them to handle according to their regulations.

. Thank You Reminders

Who to Thank and Why

Basically you want to remember and recognize people who have made a difference in your life. Often times this will boil down to anyone who serves or helps you or your family member in out of the ordinary ways or tasks. Here is a short list of the types of services that merit written thanks or more.

Nurses. Those who cared for you or your loved one during your recent hospital stay deserve a special thank you note. You might even want to send flowers or a box of chocolates to be shared by the unit staff.

Doctors. You may have placed your life in the hands of a doctor or surgeon . Show your gratitude by at least sending a note of thanks.

Teachers. Whether they be yours or your child's, the teachers in your life deserve an apple and a note of thanks. This includes the school, piano, Sunday School, art or any other teacher involved in making a difference to your child's life.

Coaches. Coaching is very difficult and often times stressful. It shows thoughtfulness on your part when you send a note at the end of the season showing your gratitude for the energy he or she has expended on behalf your child and the team.

Personal Shoppers. Thank those who put forth the extra effort of trying so hard to make your life easier. I know that Shoppers and Assistants are paid, however, they provide a very helpful service and their job quality increases as they understand just how much you appreciate them.

Housekeepers. Your domestic help should be thanked personally either with a bonus payment at some point during the year or with a heartfelt note and perhaps some candy.

Mail Delivery Persons. In rain or shine these men and women deliver our mail. Every now and again it is thoughtful to say thanks. They may not want a letter—but perhaps you could leave them some cookies or offer a drink on a hot summer day.

Vacation Hosts. Everyone knows that it is hard work playing host. If you go and visit relatives or friends and stay for any length of time while you are there you should send them a note of thanks and perhaps a gift for their hospitality. Try something like a nice houseplant or a special vase just to say 'thanks.'

These are but a few commonly overlooked thanks that I wanted to highlight. Practicing good etiquette requires that you go beyond the ordinary and do things to make life more pleasant for yourself and those around you. Etiquette demands that you behave courteously and with grace. Make it a habit to remember to thank people you have observed to be praiseworthy in their work. They will be grateful for your acknowledgement and your encouragement will pay off in their increased commitment to doing their work well.

Wittiness with Class

There is an old proverb that says that a merry heart is not only like a good medicine but, it also makes the bearer smile. Everyone loves to be amused and entertained and as a result a great deal of our time is spent in conversations and communications that contain (at least some) good humor. The ability to see humor in everyday events is certainly a great gift and it is definitely one that should be shared with others as the opportunity arises.

No one really wants to be known as the 'glass half empty' or 'pessimistic' type. So, as a well socialized individual you should definitely make an attempt to cultivate a wittiness that does not betray your class and elegance.

While you are with others you'll want to recognize that a sense of humor can be hurtful if allowed to go unchecked and untamed by manners and good sense. I'm sure that most of us have experienced the uncomfortable situation that can be caused when an attempt to be funny turns out poorly. Here are some parameters you can use in order to gauge whether or not your wittiness is appropriate or not.

Yours is a poor joke...

1. When a woman or man blushes with embarrassment as a result of what you've said. This is true in the case of children and teenagers as well. An elegant person of etiquette wants to spend their time building up others and he or she should never need to resort to matters not appropriate for G-rated audiences, especially not for the sake of a cheap laugh.
2. When someone's feelings are hurt by what you've said. In any instance that results in any of your friends or acquaintances being hurt, you should recognize that the laugh simply wasn't worth the loss of dignity you may have suffered or the pain you may have caused someone dear.
3. When something sacred is made to appear common. You should always refrain from making fun or light of someone's faith or beliefs. Even if you disagree with their position it is inappropriate for you to make fun of them. In the same way, you should always be respectful (as opposed to flippant)of clergy members and those viewed as ones who should be revered. This does not necessarily mean that you agree with their belief; but it does show that you respect him or her as an individual who has the right to hold certain items, people and beliefs as sacred or set apart.
4. When a man or woman's inability causes others to laugh. Just think, that person in the wheel chair could be you and so could the elderly gentleman using the cane. These

areas are taboo when it comes to joke material. It simply shows a lack of integrity to make light of another person's weaknesses.

5. If profanity is necessary to pull off the joke, it is an unnecessary one. A foul mouth reveals the true heart of a man or woman. Filthy and profane language is for those who lack the necessary vocabulary to speak intelligently without being crude. The person of etiquette should never be found using vulgar language--not even to spin a joke or story.

6. When a child is brought to tears by what you have said, you have said far too much. Children are to be respected just as any other human. Their frailties and lives should never be used in conversations and jokes in an effort to make others laugh.

7. When everyone can't enjoy the joke. In situations where some of those in attendance can't or were not intended to enjoy the joke, it is inappropriate. For instance, if you are in a party setting and there is a couple there from another country, it would be unkind to make joke that vilifies or belittles their native land. These are the types of judgments etiquette requires that we make constantly in order to guard ourselves from being rude.

Good humor is a great asset to have and in most circumstances the party is better off because of it. A good rule of thumb to follow would be to avoid corrupting communications which would include filthy talking and inappropriate jesting. If you use these boundaries within your communications you will be witty and stylish without losing your reputation as a class act.

What Can I Talk About During Dinner?

Determining how to choose great table topics during any dining experience may be a bit tricky. Depending upon who your dinner guests are different subjects may or may not be appropriate. As a great rule of thumb, it is best to stick with topics that are suitable and appropriate for all audiences when you are attempting to think of ways to begin and maintain lively and entertaining dinner party conversations.

Here are some more tips for making sure your guests enjoy a lively dinner-time conversation starters.

1. **Ask great questions.** It is no secret that most people (even the shy ones) like to talk about themselves--at least a little bit. Do the necessary research to show that you know some intimate details about your guests and use this information to begin a great conversation. For example: "Dr. Jewell, I understand that you spent several years working as a medical missionary in South Korea. That must have been exciting. What did you enjoy most about your experience there?" Now you smile and wait expectantly for the kind doctor to expound for several minutes about his time in South Korea. Other guests will no doubt ask other questions or begin to share their own some-how-related stories. Besides work, another great talking point is **the family.** Parents love to talk about their children, so asking questions about how they are doing is always a great option.

2. **Popular Culture Issues.** Although it is generally thought that in mixed company (meaning outside of your immediate family or normal group) it is unwise to talk politics or religion, if you choose to avoid these, talking about popular culture is a a another great way to infuse the dinner conversation. The area of pop culture opens up a plethora of options for your conversations. Just be sure to keep the conversation 'G' rated and fun. This may be accomplished by making statements about movies you recently watched or books you just read. Good magazines and travel locations are also great speaking points when it comes to conversations during dinner. Here are some starters: "I saw the best movie about baseball the other day!" "Has anyone read any good books lately?" "I was so happy to discover that the touring production of The Lion King will be coming to Illinois in March. Has your family seen the live production yet?" You should always endeavor to maintain an atmosphere that is classy rather than crude. Avoid scandalous news items and gruesome imagery such as double-homicide crime details and gossip newspaper flavored fare.

3. **Share favorite memories.** Celebratory dinners and gatherings are intended to be entertaining and fun. Try to think of some times and memorable occasions that you and your guests share and recall them as a way of enjoying your company. It is so fun to remember certain vacation fun or other events you have in common. For instance, if you all attended a special New Year's Eve ball last year, you might want to bring up some of the memorable fun you had during the event. I wouldn't suggest pulling out photos at the table, but it is certainly appropriate to offer to show photos of a certain place, person or event if your

guests inquire. This can be done after you move from the table to the family or other gathering area.

4. **Encourage others to speak.** As the host or hostess you should look for opportunities to invite those guests, who appear to be more reserved, into the conversation and fun. Your role should be to facilitate the conversations rather than dominate them. You also don't want to appear as if you are interrogating or interviewing your guests. Little phrases of invite such as, "What are your thoughts on the subject Aunt Rosalind?" will open the door and encourage those more reserved guests to weigh in on the subject at hand.

5. **Lead by example.** Your attitude and behavior are crucial to the success or failure of your dinner party event. You could say that with you it either rises or falls. If you are upbeat, positive, joyful and pleasant, you will go a long way toward setting your guests at ease. In a comfortable atmosphere your friends, family and associates will share and participate more freely than they would were you to seem stressed or tired. Be sure to get a good night's sleep before the party and receive your guest in a refreshed mood prepared to have a great time of fellowship together.

Author

Robin A. Bickerstaff Glover is a committed Christian wife, mother, business woman, coach and friend. She is a commissioned Missionary who has served as a pastor/teacher/evangelist's wife for over a decade. Robin is a graduate of Liberty University with multi-disciplinary degrees in Religion and Communications. She is a member of the American Association of Christian Counselors and is a Certified Christian Life Coach. Her coaching studies were through Light University and Liberty University.

Robin is a graduate of the John Robert Powers Finishing and modeling school and is the former etiquette expert for About.com, the New York Time's online information resource site. Robin is the co-owner and co-founder of Christian Graces, LLC and its subsidiaries including Channels of Grace and CG Publishing.

Robin is married to Evangelist/Missionary Steven A. Glover, and she is the mom to four daughters: Gabe, Noah, Jewell and Selah. The family currently resides in Toledo, Ohio where they are members of Emmanuel Baptist Church.

Robin is also an accomplished Christian vocal artist and she is available for women's retreats, teas and conferences as either a speaker or worship leader.

Contact info: www.christiangraces.com or robin@christiangraces.com